STAGGERED
PATHS

STRANGE DEATHS IN THE BADGER STATE

Badger Wordsmith, LLC
Published in Wales, Wisconsin

STEVEN SPINGOLA

STAGGERED PATHS: STRANGE DEATHS IN THE BADGER STATE

The author has done his best to present accurate and relevant information in this book. In instances where an opinion or speculation is offered, these views and opinions, unless attributed, are solely those of Steven Spingola.

ISBN: 978-0-692-91013-9

Author: Steven Spingola

STAGGERED PATHS: STRANGE DEATHS IN THE BADGER STATE (2nd Editon)

Steven Spingola

Twitter: @MilwSpinny

Crimes and offenses—United States—non-fiction

CONTENTS

PROLOGUE

In the wee hours of April 27, 2015, thirty-two-year old Robin Krabill staggered into an alley in the rear of the 100 block of 3rd Street South, a trendy area of shops and taverns in downtown La Crosse, Wisconsin. The 1998 Waterloo, Iowa, High School graduate ran with a tough crowd and frequently hurled expletives. "Thank u to bae n his fam," an earlier post on Krabill's Facebook page noted, "they made me feel welcome [in La Crosse] n glad i came n of course fuck the haters im not goin anywhere so get use to seein this bitch!!!!!"[1]

Krabill's crude rant proved rather ironic. At 4 a.m., a surveillance camera captured an image of the woman as she struggled to climb a three-story fire escape behind Digger's Sting. Unable to enter a secured door, Krabill slowly descended down the metal steps, lost her balance, tumbled over a railing, and plummeted to her death. Her bloody corpse was discovered three hours later by the store's co-owner.[2]

No doubt, the watchful eye of a surveillance camera saved investigators countless hours. Without the video, Krabill's death would have likely been classified as suspicious. Detectives would want to know why the woman climbed the fire escape. Was she being chased by someone? Was she engaged in some sort of domestic spat? Was she pushed over the railing? Absent the video footage, law enforcement would have undoubtedly scrutinized some of the dead woman's friends and associates.

After a toxicology report pegged Krabill's blood alcohol content at 0.24, three times the legal limit to drive, La Crosse police closed the case as an accidental death due, in part, to acute alcohol intoxication.[3]

Robin Krabill's staggered path is unfortunately too often traveled. Whether young people fall from fire escapes or drown in bodies of water, excessive alcohol consumption is the Badger State's most prolific serial killer. Wisconsin resident John Schaus ought to know. The eight-time convicted drunk driver has gone eleven years without catching another case. "To avoid the temptation of ever drinking and driving again," reporter John Ferak noted, "Schaus no longer drives or owns an automobile."[4]

"There's a mindset in Wisconsin," said Schaus. "There's even a T-shirt that says "Drink Wisconsinbly." While on a cruise with one hundred and twenty other cheeseheads, Schaus was approached by a man from another state. "You guys from Wisconsin drink like you're nuts," said the man. "They should put a fence around the place and send in a bunch of psychiatrists." During the seven-day excursion, the cruise's revelers "drank the boat out of light beer."[5]

The Badger State's hard-drinking reputation is a stark reality. Still, it seems, too many decent, well-educated people are in denial. At summer cookouts or during social events, I am sometimes asked if a serial killer is on the loose in Wisconsin college towns. "After all," said one woman, "all these college kids drowning can't possibly be happenstance."

Some people apparently believe there is no such thing as a coincidence. Any objective investigator worth his or her detective's badge would, of course, disagree. In my book, *Best of the Spingola Files, Volumes 1 & 2*, I profiled the bizarre saga of the "Honeybee Shooter," where a series of coincidences resulted in an innocent man being jailed on murder charges.

In early October of 2010, a middle-aged man approached a group of construction workers in the rural town of Beecher, Illinois. For no apparent reason, the stranger shot and killed one of the construction workers and wounded another. Less than an hour later, the same individual visited a farm in the rural community of Lowell, Indiana, inquired about honeybees being kept on the property, then shot the farmer for no apparent reason. The perpetrator fled in a light colored pick-up truck.[6]

Officials from the Will County, Illinois, Sheriff's Department released a physical description of the suspect and the truck. An hour later, off-duty Lynwood, Illinois, police officer Brian Dorian was stopped because "his truck matched the description of the vehicle — a white or silver Chevrolet pickup truck — mentioned in an all-points bulletin." Dorian, whose physical description was similar to the shooter's, identified himself as an off-duty police officer. He was briefly questioned and released.[7]

Later, the Schererville police officer who had stopped Dorian was shown a composite sketch of the suspect and told investigators that the shooter was "the guy" he had stopped in the aftermath of the shooting in Lowell, Indiana.[8]

"We put it in a six pack, a lineup of six people, and took it to the victim witness [the third worker at the construction site]," said Will

County Sheriff Paul Kaupas. "And we asked him, 'Does anybody on there look familiar?' and he said, 'Yes,' and we said, 'Who?' and he pointed to (Dorian's) photograph but stated, 'He looks older now.'"[9]

Detectives staked out Dorian's residence. When the off-duty officer left his home, investigators questioned a "lady friend," who said the officer's truck was at a local repair shop getting outfitted with a new set of tires. The sheriff believed Dorian had destroyed evidence. "We knew that day that Lake County had shown some kind of a news reel about them trying to take imprints of the tire tracks out at their shooting scene."[10]

When contacted by authorities, Dorian chose to cooperate with investigators. He was, however, unable to provide critical details about his activities days earlier. "You have all this circumstantial stuff and he won't tell you ... what he's doing," said a Will County Sheriff's spokesman. "And all Dorian would say is that he was watching TV— and no further explanation." Dorian's cellular provider reported that the off-duty officer's telephone "showed he was near Cedar Lake," a location six-and-a-half miles south of Lowell, Indiana, and fourteen miles east of Beecher, Illinois, on the day of the shootings.[11]

On October 8, Dorian was arrested. At a line up inside the county jail, witnesses identified the off-duty officer as the perpetrator. Dorian was charged with murder and his bail was set at $2.5 million. Taking the government's findings at face value, the media explored the officer's background, interviewed family and friends, and scrutinized Dorian's Facebook page.[12]

In the aftermath of the officer's arrest, I expressed a certain skepticism in a blog post at the *Spingola Files*. The officer's allegedly bizarre conduct made no sense. Why would a man who, for the most part, had led an exemplary life suddenly shoot people for no apparent reason? Absent mental health issues or substance intoxication, an individual's propensity for violence usually increases over time. According to co-workers, as well as the officer who had conducted the vehicle stop, Dorian was mentally fit and sober when the shootings occurred.[13]

The case fell apart in late October when forensic investigators searched the off-duty officer's computer. During an interrogation, Dorian explained that, on the date of the shooting, he had spent some time on the Internet. The sheriff told the media "someone was using the computer at 10:25 a.m. on sites that require passwords." The first shooting occurred in Beecher at 10:30 a.m., which meant Dorian would have had to travel sixteen-and-a-half miles in five minutes. Ballistics also showed the rounds used in the shootings did not match the firearms possessed by the off-duty officer. Still, the cloud of suspicion threatened to derail Dorian's career.[14]

On November 18, an individual using the moniker "Louis 31" challenged the *Spingola Files'* defense of the formerly jailed cop. The poster offered specific details concerning the circumstantial evidence and lamented that "anyone" could have logged-in to the computer, even though the passwords belonged to accounts that Dorian had established.[15]

Just three weeks later, a botched armed robbery at an Orlando Park, Illinois, LA Tan salon debunked the arguments of "Louis 31." While in the process of binding a customer's hands and feet, the perpetrator was disarmed by a man with martial arts experience, who then shot and killed the robber. The deceased was identified as forty-eight-year-old Gary Amaya, of Rankin, Illinois. Amaya's physical description and the blue Chevrolet pick-up truck he owned bore a striking resemblance to the honeybee shooter. A ballistics test linked Amaya's gun to the shootings in Illinois and Indiana.[16]

Coincidences do occur, which is why it is important to objectively evaluate evidence. As a rookie cop, a veteran colleague instructed me to keep an open mind. "I've been sent to parking troubles that were shootings," the officer related, "and been dispatched to shootings that turned out to be parking troubles. So don't make the mistake of prejudging a situation before you get there."

Consequently, when a decision was made to review the strange deaths of young men in the Badger State, I did so with an open mind. Amateur sleuths, along with some of the family members of those who had perished, have asserted that something is amiss and a killer is at large. On the other hand, investigators from various law enforcement agencies confidentially state the perpetrator is a man of high rank — Captain Morgan.

As I combed through the newspaper accounts and police reports of thirty deaths, alcohol consumption played some sort of role in ninety percent of the cases. In one La Crosse incident, homicide charges could be issued if a suspect is positively identified. In another instance, the demise of a troubled man in Green Bay merits further investigation. Two other death investigations offered more questions than answers and a few others contained unexplainable gaps in time.

As technology advanced, video surveillance and cellular telephone tracking resulted in fewer investigative timeline fissures. Within the span of a few years, detectives in jurisdictions with a rash of strange deaths had a better grasp of available resources. This pattern can certainly be seen in La Crosse.

It is, however, the story behind the story that stands out in some of the otherwise clear-cut, accidental deaths. All of us have our secrets, as do our family members and friends. Yet, when an otherwise healthy person suddenly dies, a law enforcement probe can expose a host of embarrassing information, such as over-the-top drug abuse, sexual liaisons, and charlatanism.

The premise of this book is to prove or disprove the presence of a shadowy serial killer — a man or woman, or possibly a group of psychopaths, that lures intoxicated young men to their perditions. To do so, I saw no need to explain that a deceased person was a fan of NASCAR, enjoyed writing hip-hop lyrics or maintained a close relationship with his parents, unless, of course, these personality traits were somehow relevant to their deaths. To complete this book, I have combed through more than a thousand pages of police reports and dozens of newspaper articles. Having spent fifteen years as a homicide detective, I parlayed what I saw as the important details of each investigation into the pages of *Staggered Paths*. The end result is a book that reads like a police report and cuts to the chase of the tome's overall premise.

CHAPTER ONE
DEATH OF A FRESHMAN

While speaking with members of the public or media, I am occasionally asked about the criteria used for labeling a death "suspicious." Though each investigation is unique, a suspicious death is generally one that, due to the age and/or health of the deceased, lacks an explanation other than the involvement of another party.

Suspicious deaths come in a variety of forms, such as drownings, drug overdoses, alleged suicides, and poisonings. Drownings are deaths by asphyxiation caused by liquid inhalation, which prohibits oxygen from getting to the brain. In cold water, the onset of hypothermia may result in drowning.[1]

At the scene of a drowning, investigators look for typical and atypical factors. In many instances, vomit will be present in the mouth of the individual who died immersed in water. Another indicator of a drowning death is foam emanating from the mouth and nose of the deceased, which illustrates that the victim became immersed while still conscious and breathing. If a foam-like substance is not present in the mouth and nose, the individual was likely intoxicated or unconscious when they entered the water.[2]

Since drowning is the fourth leading cause of accidental death in the United States, divers, investigators, and pathologists have substantial experience probing water immersion deaths. One critical factor is the location of post mortem lividity on the body.

Divers report that submerged corpses usually assume a "prone, semi-fetal position." In these situations, the head tends to lunge forward and the back is bent somewhat upward. Therefore, lividity — a condition caused when gravity pulls the deceased's bodily fluids to their lowest resting point — is usually found in the head. If, for example, a drowning victim was discovered submerged in the prone position and lividity was found on the back, this condition would suggest that the body was placed in a lake or river after death had occurred.[3]

Whether a drowning death is classified an accident, a suicide or homicide often depends on the evidence found inside or about the body, as well as the individual's activities prior to their demise. In some instances, gaps in a victim's investigative timeline make a cause of death determination an inexact science.

The death of Stephan Kappell is a prime example of a suspicious death. One can only speculate about the risks and decisions assumed by the eighteen-year-old Kaukauna, Wisconsin, native, whose square jaw, brush haircut, and black framed glasses punctuated his six-foot-two, two-hundred-and-ten pound muscular frame. Kappell played high school football and was also involved in a number of extracurricular activities. After enrolling at the Wisconsin State University at Oshkosh for the fall 1965 semester, he became a backup center for the football team. During his first three weeks on campus, Kappell quietly blended in with the rest of the primarily white, middle-class freshmen.[4]

Things changed on Tuesday, September 28th, at about 6 p.m. Kappell was observed leaving Breeze Hall, a tan brick dormitory nestled near Nelson and Clemens resident halls. Two days later, when a friend from Kaukauna arrived on campus for a visit, Kappell was nowhere to be found. Initially, authorities believed the missing student was homesick and may have returned to his parent's residence, but he never arrived. Soon afterwards, a missing person's report was filed with the Kaukauna Police Department.[5]

On October 15, the *Oshkosh Northwestern* ran a story about the still missing freshman, and noted that the Outagamie County Sheriff's Department was asked to assist with the investigation. The following day, a human body floated to the surface in Lake Winnebago's Miller Bay. Oshkosh Symphony Conductor Harold Arentsen, who was fishing in the cove, spotted a bloated corpse and contacted the police. When the fire department pulled the body to shore near Hickory Street, investigators noticed the dead man was naked and his face badly bruised. The man's hands and knees had been bound with "tan-colored heavy ribbed cotton" cloth, consistent with a type of athletic bandage used in the 1960s and 1970s. Thirty-four centimeters of this cloth separated each hand and was knotted in the middle. A sling or noose, comprised of similar, but multiple strips of cloth material, was attached to a thirty-pound rock and bound with similar ligatures to Kappell's feet.[6]

Two days later, Oshkosh police used fingerprints to identify the dead man as Kappell. Since eighteen-year-olds are rarely fingerprinted for employment or administrative purposes, the identification of body vis-à-vis fingerprints strongly suggests Kappell may have had a run-in with the law as a juvenile. This observation seemed to go unnoticed by the press.[7]

On October 17, an autopsy was performed at the Milwaukee County Morgue by Assistant Medical Examiner Helen Young, who noted that "Mr. Kappell died of drowning and, that prior to his death, had sustained trauma to the head." Young further noted the body had been in the water approximately three weeks, which is consistent with the time period when he first went missing. This finding, coupled with the body being found nude, bound, and weighted, seemed to suggest foul play. The strap used to attach the thirty-pound rock to Kappell's feet had a "double metal loop" and "on the external surface of this webbed stamp are the poorly defined number38." Although the notes in the autopsy report are vague, it appears that the number 38 was handwritten, as if the bandaging was associated with the number of an athletic jersey.[8]

On December 8, a coroner's inquest jury heard testimony concerning the cause of Kappell's death in Oshkosh. Young told the jury that the eighteen-year old was likely conscious when entering the water, but then struck an object once in the lake.[9]

"Was Stephan Kappell, the likable, polite, husky athlete and ardent fisherman, murdered?" asked a front-page article in the *Neenah-Menasha Northwestern*. "Or was Stephan Kappell, the insecure, emerging-from-adolescence young man plagued with self-doubt, driven to self-destruction." The coroner's inquest heard ten hours of testimony but took just twenty minutes to declare it could not decide if the death was a suicide or a homicide.[10]

The jury verdict was not necessarily shocking; however, the inquest failed to answer several key questions. Kappell had resided in Oshkosh for less than a month. The area where his body was found — Miller's Bay, in Lake Winnebago — is almost two-and-a-half miles from campus. If he committed suicide, Kappell either procured a boat or walked a long stretch of breakwater — visible from the residential area on shore — while naked and toting a thirty-pound rock. A suicide theory fails to account for the lack of an unoccupied boat on the lake or the whereabouts of Kappell's clothing near shore. According to the coroner's report and newspaper accounts, no suicide note was left behind. Moreover, Kappell was in good spirits during a stay at home, which concluded just two days before he went missing. During this visit, the freshman told his family he "enjoyed every minute" of his time at college.[11]

The location of the drowning is also suspect. If Kappell sought to commit suicide, why did he travel two-and-a-half miles when the Fox River abuts the UW – Oshkosh campus directly to the west?

Soon, rumors swirled Kappell had committed suicide. After his body was found in Miller's Bay, a member of the football team, Dan Buhr, vaguely recalled hearing that a co-ed had ended her brief relationship with Kappell. "Through the rumor mill," said Buhr, word spread the freshman had "jumped from a boat with a rock tied to him."[12]

Prior to the coroner's inquest, the press reviewed a handful of other strange deaths in the Fox River Valley area. One unsolved homicide involved a twenty-one-year-old female clerk who was stabbed fifty-three times in the back at a gas station on U.S. Highway 41. Still, the *modus operandi* in the solved and unsolved cases were different than the circumstances surrounding Stephan Kappell's drowning death.[13]

What about the presence of the number "38," which was etched into the cotton bandaging stamp used to bind Kappell's hands and feet? Did investigators bother to check out this valuable piece of physical evidence? Unfortunately, we may never know. In 2014, when Kappell's sister contacted the Oshkosh Police Department for a status update, police officials learned that the reports had gone missing.[14]

Although it is impossible to know for sure, it is reasonable to suspect investigators explored a link to the number 38 and a logical place to start was the football team.

A photocopied roster of the 1965 Wisconsin State University at Oshkosh football team indicates that the number "38" was unassigned; however, the team photograph that year, which did not include or mention Kappell, oddly depicts the players in their practice jerseys. Some of the visible practice jersey numbers in this photo do not correspond to the numbers on the official team roster. It is, therefore, possible that the number 38 may be connected to a practice jersey and not a roster jersey.[15]

With the police reports missing, one can only speculate as to the significance investigators gave to the number 38. Yet if detectives relied on the numbers listed on the team roster, and not those associated with the practice jerseys, it is possible an important piece of information may have gone unnoticed.

Still, one could reasonably suspect that Kappell, who was assigned jersey number 52, left his dorm at 6 p.m. on September 28, 1965, to visit a person(s) he knew. Having been on campus less than a month, a likelihood exists that the last person to see the eighteen-year-old alive was someone he knew.

Kappell's disappearance is a prime example of a suspicious death, which is why I chose to examine this older case first. In fact, an employee of the Winnebago County Coroner's Office related that the television program *Unsolved Mysteries* had previously requested the deceased freshman's autopsy reports. Depending on the quality of packaging and/or the existence of the physical evidence recovered during autopsy (i.e. the cotton bandaging), DNA evidence may still be available. Yet it is unclear where this evidence is stored or if it even exists. This question could be answered by an extensive search of evidence lockers and other documents maintained by the Oshkosh Police Department.

In the Kappell case, the totality of the still existing record points to a homicide, not a suicide. When conducting criminal investigations, detectives seek to answer the who, what, when, where, why, and how questions. Typically, an answer to the "why" question is not required for most prosecutions. Yet, to ascertain the answer to the "who" question in Kappell's death, an investigator would likely need to determine why the crime was committed.

Absent police reports, it is challenging, but not impossible, to construct a theory or theories for a crime. Having been trained in criminal investigative analysis (i.e. criminal profiling) at the FBI academy, I can tell you the setting where a crime is committed is sometimes telling. Kappell's death either occurred, or was arranged on or near a college campus, where an individual who played football or pledged to a fraternity, in the mid-1960s, may have been subjected to physical abuse. Besides the severe bruising to his face, however, Kappell did not sustain injuries — welts/bruising to the buttocks or back of the legs — consistent with hazing.

College campus environments also are facilitators for sexual experimentation. A student's stay on or near campus means independence from the watchful eyes of their parents and other family members. In some instances, though, an unassuming freshman, especially one who is seeking to fit in and make new friends, may learn that "friendship" means different things to different people.

Although historians often describe the 1960s as a period of youthful "idealism, protest, and rebellion," societal attitudes towards homosexuality, even amongst college students, were rooted in post-World War II American traditionalism. "Beset by inner conflicts," an article from a 1966 edition of *Time* magazine notes, "the homosexual is unsure of his position in society, ambivalent about his attitudes and identity — but he gains a certain amount of security through the fact that society is equally ambivalent about him. A vast majority of people retain a deep loathing toward him, but there is a growing mixture of tolerance, empathy or apathy."[16]

In the 1960s, same sex relationships often occurred under a cloak of secrecy. There were few, if any gay night clubs, especially in Wisconsin's Fox River Valley area. As a result, it was much more difficult for young gay men to identify those with similar proclivities.

In his book, *The World Turned: Essays on Gay History, Politics, and Culture*, John D'Emilio describes his 1960s search for other gay men as a process of "trial and error," which consisted of meeting men in parks or on balconies of theaters, and having sex in alleys or public toilets. D'Emilio always used an alias and rarely had sex with the same man more than once out of fear that doing so "would be a route to exposure."[17]

Fifty-two years ago, there were very few venues for gay men, such as those described by D'Emilio, in Oshkosh. Thus, the "trial and error" process used to identify potential lovers increased the risk of "exposure." In many instances, being uncovered meant societal marginalization, a limited career track, and conflict with family and friends. For example, if a gay man hoped to become an engineer and gain employment with a company that did work for the U.S. Department of Defense, "exposure" could result in a security clearance being denied. During this period, for example, one could only imagine the social stigma attached to an exposed gay member(s) of the football team.

If Kappell rejected a "trial and error" sexual advance and appeared indignant while doing so, an individual(s) fearing the social stigma of exposure might lash out. One example is the 2005 Missouri trial of off-duty police officer Steven Rios, who was convicted of killing his gay lover. The body of a University of Missouri student, Jesse Valencia, was discovered on a green space near the campus in Columbia. Valencia's throat was cut so deep and so thoroughly that marks from the edged weapon were located on his spine.[18]

Valencia "told classmates he suspected his new lover was married and planned to confront him," wrote *CourtTV* reporter Harriet Ryan. "He also wanted Rios to fix the ticket from the party and suggested to his best friend he would tell the chief of his "little secret" if the ticket didn't go away."[19]

In 2005, societal views of same sex relationships were much more tolerant than those of 1965. Still, the stigma of being linked to a sexual scandal resulted in a very violent and heinous murder.

In regards to the Kappell case, my inquiry unearthed some information that supports the foundation for this hypothesis. The passage of time, however, has made it extremely difficult to prove or disprove critical details. Nonetheless, a strong likelihood exists that, if Stephan Kappell was killed, the suspect was a white male, between the ages of eighteen and twenty-three, who was strong and athletic.

CHAPTER TWO
LA CROSSE BEGINNINGS

La Crosse, Wisconsin is a blue collar town situated along a beautiful stretch of the Mississippi River. From the bluffs on the east side of the city, visitors can see the campus of the University of Wisconsin – La Crosse. The hard drinking college crowd typically congregates in the city's downtown area, where taverns dot locations on Third, Fourth, Main and Pearl Streets. Although the campus is just a mile and a half northwest of the city's entertainment district, inebriated people, for whatever reasons, seem to make the quarter-mile trek east to the banks of the mighty Mississippi.

Since 1997, the lives of twelve young men ended after falling into the rivers near La Crosse. These individuals had two things in common: All were less that twenty-five years-old and, prior to their deaths, each engaged in heavy bouts of binge drinking. Some observers suspect — absent any qualitative evidence — that the sheer number of drowning deaths suggests a serial killer is trolling the streets on the lookout for intoxicated men to push into the river.

Though quantitative data alone may suffice to formulate a hypothesis, an analysis of these drownings — not just in La Crosse, but in other areas of Wisconsin — calls for a sufficient examination of each death on a case-by-case basis. The first case, in what conspiracy theorists claim is a trend, is the death of Richard Hlavaty.

On Thursday, July 10, 1997, nineteen-year-old Richard traveled from his family's home in Western Springs, Illinois, to visit his brother, James Hlavaty, who was a student at UW – La Crosse. The following evening, the Hlavaty brothers, along with a friend, Ryan Feggestad, began drinking beer around 9 p.m. at a home on Pine Street, just a mile and a half west of the downtown entertainment district. The three men later traveled to Yesterday's Pub in the 300 block of Pearl Street. Under twenty-one years of age, Richard used a forged Michigan identification card of his alias, Bryan Connelly, of 295 Harvard Street, in Kalamazoo, to gain entrance into the tavern.[20]

A short time thereafter, the Hlavatys and Feggestad walked across the street to Brother's Pub, where they stayed until bar closing time. After leaving Brother's, the three men strode west towards Third Street and observed an altercation taking place on the corner. Although he did not know any of the parties involved, Richard intervened, sought to break up the ensuing fight, and was punched. James then entered the crowd and struck the man he believed had hit his brother. The individual punched by the six-feet-two, two-hundred-ten pound James Hlavaty — Christopher "Critter" Poehling — was knocked unconscious and fell to the ground.[21]

Unknown to the Hlavatys, a large contingent of Critter's friends were present. Upset by the perceived cheap shot, eight or nine men began chasing the brothers south on Pearl Street and west on Jay Street towards the Mississippi River. Apparently more of a lover than a fighter, Feggestad kept a safe distance, remained on the corner of Third and Pearl Streets, and looked on as the Hlavatys ran for their lives.[22]

At the end of Front Street, the Hlavaty brothers continued south, ran past the Courtyard by Marriott Hotel, and under a freeway overpass that adjoined three grain elevators and the Mississippi River. As Richard entered the river, James was confronted by several men who began to beat him. In an effort to avoid being pummeled, James jumped down onto a pile of rocks adjacent to the river and, in the process, was injured when he fell. Fearing for his safety, James entered the water and began swimming away from shore. While in the water, Richard shouted he was going to swim across the river.[23]

Having yet to avenge Critter's beating, the men on shore began to throw large, tennis ball-sized rocks at their now swimming targets. As the swift current carried him downstream, James deflected some of the incoming rocks with his arm. When exiting the water two blocks to the south at Division Street, James spotted a trucker parked near La Crosse Plumbing. The trucker agreed to give James a ride to Feggestad's apartment, located at 511 Cass Street. After retrieving a dry set of clothes, James Hlavaty and Feggestad traveled to the Holiday Inn Hotel, a few blocks from where the brothers had entered the river. Feggestad made contact with a hotel employee, Dustin Mueller, and asked if he had observed a person who was "all wet" enter the hotel. Mueller contacted the La Crosse Police Department, and Officers Ronald Secord and Rick

Pfennig were sent to investigate.[24]

During an interview with Pfenning, James Hlavaty told an officer that, although he and his brother were drinking at the house, Richard did not have much to drink at Brother's Pub. Nearly four hours after his brother went missing, James consented to a preliminary breath test and registered a blood alcohol content of 0.167. When Pfenning advised James he may want to contact his father about the matter, James replied, "No, I don't want him to know anything yet."[25]

Although deputies from the La Crosse County Sheriff's Department searched the river by boat, over a day passed before the La Crosse Fire Department located a body in the Mississippi River. On July 13, at 11:30 a.m., Richard Hlavaty's corpse was brought ashore at the foot of Division Street — the same location where James Hlavaty had climbed ashore a day and half earlier.[26]

The body was transported to the St. Francis morgue and placed on an examination table. Richard was still attired in the same clothing — a red and black button-down shirt and blue jeans — that he sported on the morning of his disappearance. After photographing the body, Medical Examiner Ron Uber drew blood, took an X-ray, and noted the deceased's body temperature was 84 degrees.[27]

After Richard's clothing was removed, the body was examined by Uber and a La Crosse PD investigator, who observed "pronounced lividity in the upper chest area, shoulders, and especially in the face and head." This would suggest the deceased's head was downward and the legs were in a more upright position. Richard's right arm had a rather large, one-and-a-half inch abrasion under the forearm and another two-inch abrasion on the side of the elbow. These injuries may have stemmed from deflecting thrown rocks or by striking the right arm on an object while entering the water.[28]

Other wounds included swelling around Richard's right eye, which would suggest he may have been punched by a left-handed person. There was some minor swelling to the left eye, which was less pronounced. The deceased's left elbow had a two-inch abrasion. Abrasions were also present on both knees.[29]

After learning of the foot chase and rock throwing, La Crosse County District Attorney Scott Horne ordered Richard's body be transported to

Madison for an autopsy. Toxicology tests later revealed Richard's blood alcohol content was 0.271, almost three-and-a-half times over the limit to legally drive.[30]

On July 14, Richard's body was conveyed to the Veterans Administration Hospital in Madison, where an autopsy revealed that the cause of death was drowning; however, the manner of death was listed as "undetermined." While at the autopsy, an attending detective further observed an injury to the "back of the head" of Richard and another injury to the forehead area. Dr. Huntington, the physician in charge of the proceeding, noted some hemorrhaging had occurred in these areas, but "no skull fracture that could be observed." The abrasions sustained to Richard's arms and legs, in the doctor's opinion, were sustained prior to his death.[31]

Since rocks had been thrown towards the brothers while in the river, and with Richard's head bearing some unexplainable hemorrhaging of blood, the La Crosse Police Department correctly investigated the incident as a possible homicide.

On the same morning the autopsy was performed, Christopher "Critter" Poehling voluntarily appeared at the La Crosse Police Department. While being interviewed by detectives, Poehling said he had been drinking at Sneaker's tavern and met an "English girl," who was a foreign exchange student. After leaving the pub at closing time, he walked to the area of Third and Pearl Streets, where a small crowd had gathered. Someone in the crowd "flicked off" his hat. Poehling turned around and said to the man behind him, "Hey, dude, did you see my hat?" When he turned his head forward, another man punched Poehling in the face and knocked him out. When he awoke, the parties involved in the foot pursuit were gone.[32]

Soon afterwards, investigators caught a break. At 11:30 a.m., Detective Dunham received a telephone call from an "anonymous female," who had heard of the Hlavaty drowning. The female related that two men, Carl Moore and Hilton Riggins, were present when the Hlavaty brothers entered the water. The caller alleged Higgins was "throwing rocks at the parties who were in the water."[33]

Two hours later, Detective Dunham and a La Crosse PD sergeant located Moore, who admitted he and his cousin, Hilton Higgins, were in the area of Third and Pearl Streets on the morning of Richard Hlavaty's death. According to Moore, after observing a fight on the corner, he witnessed four white males chasing the Hlavaty brothers westward and followed the pursuit. Once at the foot of the river, Moore said some "white guys" threw rocks at the two men in the water.[34]

Later that afternoon, Dunham located University of Wisconsin – La Crosse student Hilton Riggins, who admitted being present at the river and being friends with "Critter," who had been knocked unconscious. Although he was "upset" that his friend had been beaten, Higgins denied throwing any rocks.[35]

Another man involved in the pursuit, Phillip Neitz, had contacted a La Crosse lawyer, who arranged for a police interview of his client. If this attorney believed Neitz was in any way culpable for the rock throwing, he would have likely advised his client to remain silent.[36]

Interviewed by Dunham at police headquarters, Neitz indicated his friend, Jesse Miller, was involved in an unrelated tussle outside of Brother's Pub just after bar time on July 12. Afterwards, he and Miller observed the fight on Third and Pearl Streets and followed the pursuit of the Hlavaty brothers. After one of the brothers was in the water, Neitz saw "one black guy," who had on an orange shirt, "throwing rocks at the guy in the water." Since Miller was closer to the action near the river, Neitz asked his friend what had transpired; whereby, Miller, a former UW — La Crosse football player, allegedly replied, "You don't want to know." Although Neitz did observe large rocks being thrown and heard them enter the water, he denied throwing any rocks and said he was not involved in any physical altercation.[37]

Confronted with several conflicting statements, investigators from the La Crosse Police Department believed some type of criminal conduct occurred prior to the drowning death of Richard Hlavaty; however, it was difficult to discern precisely who was responsible and how many individuals were culpable. While chasing the men to the river would not, by itself, constitute a felony, if one of the thrown rocks had knocked Richard Hlavaty unconscious and, therefore, resulted in his drowning death, a charge of reckless homicide may have been appropriate.

In the early 1990s, a similar case occurred during my tenure as a homicide detective. After an argument under Milwaukee's Hoan Bridge near Lake Michigan, a man was chased by several others, one of whom allegedly fired a gun shot. Fearing for his life, the fleeing man jumped into the water and drowned. Similar to the Hlavaty investigation, witnesses gave conflicting statements. As a result, the Milwaukee County District Attorney's office declined to pursue criminal charges.

As was the case in Milwaukee, the investigation into Richard Hlavaty's death turned cold. In 2013, new information surfaced. A citizen, who requested to remain anonymous, told investigators a man she had been dating related that his close friend had thrown rocks into the river on the morning Richard had drown.[38]

La Crosse PD Detective Ryan Fitzgerald diligently tracked down the alleged suspect, who resided near Madison, Wisconsin. Over the course of a few months, Fitzgerald sought to arrange an interview with the man, who claimed he had sold cars to "eighty Madison police officers, is friends with many of them, and would be embarrassed if they saw him walk" into a Madison police station to be interviewed."[39]

Although he denied being involved or present on the banks of the Mississippi River when the Hlavaty brothers entered the water, as of January 2014, the alleged suspect has refused to return any of Fitzgerald's telephone calls.[40]

The death of Richard Hlavaty took another bizarre twist in April 2014. In an effort to jump-start the investigation, Detective Fitzgerald left at least five telephone messages on Hlavaty's answering machine, but no response was received.[41]

Fitzgerald referred his findings to the La Crosse County District Attorney's office in April 2014. The county's district attorney, Tim Gruenke, asked for the file and indicated he would consider conducting a John Doe probe — a secret, fact finding court inquiry overseen by a judge. In such a hearing, individuals are compelled to provide testimony. As of this writing, however, it is unclear if such a hearing has been conducted.[42]

What is clear, however, is a serial killer was not responsible for Hlavaty's death, which is why it is important to analyze each case in its own totality.

Blatz Signs

Just two-and-a-half months after the Hlavaty drowning, two incidents raised the specter that something was awry in La Crosse. Both of the incidents involved binge drinking and college-age men.

On Friday, September 26, 1997, Charles Blatz and fellow UW — Platteville student Matt Elskamp arrived in La Crosse for the city's annual Oktoberfest celebration. The two men had made arrangements to stay at a flat rented, in part, by Matt's cousin, Tony Elskamp.[43]

That evening, the three men left the flat and ventured downtown. At some point they split up, and Blatz was able to find his way back to the flat, located at 220 N. 9th Street. The following evening, after drinking off-and-on since the late afternoon, the three men again left Elskamp's place and ventured into La Crosse's downtown entertainment district. At about 12:30 a.m., Blatz indicated he was leaving Sneaker's Bar and would return to Happenings Tap, a bar the trio had previously visited. It was the last time the Elskamp's would see Blatz alive.[44]

When Blatz failed to return to the 9th Street address, the cousins began to worry. Two days passed before they made contact with Blatz's parents. On September 30, Blatz's father, Glenroy, reported his son missing to the Kiel Police Department, the locale where the family resided. Officers from the La Crosse Police Department soon conducted a canvas of a number of downtown drinking establishments, including Coconut Joe's, Sneaker's, the Swing Inn, Digger's Bar and the Happenings Tap. Since Blatz was from out-of-town and unfamiliar to the bartenders or bouncers, none of those interviewed recalled Blatz visiting their businesses.[45]

Blatz's mother, Henrietta, told investigators her son — a military veteran and engineering major at UW — Platteville — had indicated that, though his studies were sometimes difficult, he "seemed to be doing okay." Approximately nine months prior to his disappearance, Charles broke off an engagement with his fiancé and, according to his mother, had "handled the break up very well." While her son did drink, Blatz's mother was adamant he did not use drugs. Since it was unlike Charles to disappear for days at a time, Mrs. Blatz told police her son was likely not "alive at this time." Armed with this information, police again searched garbage dumpsters, parking ramps and vacant businesses, as well as a long stretch of the banks of the Mississippi River, but found nothing.[46]

Then, on October 3, just after 8 a.m., La Crosse police received a call concerning a body floating in the main channel of the Mississippi River. The La Crosse Fire Department soon located and recovered the body near the municipal boat landing, less than a mile-and-a-half from Happenings Tap. Aboard the fire department's boat, an officer observed the body, which was located straight west of the landing, face down in the water. The top-third of the corpse's head had been severed, and a portion of the right arm, from the elbow to the fingers, was missing. After being transported to shore by the fire department, the body was transported to the St. Francis Medical Center morgue.[47]

A day later, duck hunter Peter Jerwoski parked his boat near the shore just to the north of the Marco Road municipal boat launch. When he stood up, Jerwoski observed a human arm along the river's shoreline. Assistant Medical Examiner Mary Lou Hatfield responded to the scene, retrieved the arm, and transported it to the St. Francis morgue. The limb was placed next to the body.[48]

When the corpse arrived at the St. Francis morgue, the medical examiner made contact with a physician, who conducted a cursory examination of the deceased. Attired in a purple/maroon polo shirt and blue jeans, the clothing matched the last known description of Blatz. Still in a rear pants pocket was a wallet containing Blatz's identification. Due to a lack of any hemorrhaging on the head and arm, Porter was of the opinion the injuries "occurred post-mortem."[49]

On October 6, Blatz's body was transported to the Milwaukee County Medical Examiner's office for an autopsy. Again, the physician in charge of the proceeding, Dr. Kenneth Stormo, noted there was "no sign of hemorrhage at any of the injury sites" and, therefore, concluded the injuries occurred post-mortem. Dr. Stormo determined the "likely" cause of death was drowning. An internal examination of the body revealed Blatz had also sustained blunt force trauma to the spine, which, after being severed, perforated the chest cavity. The fractured thrashing from the severed spine caused noticeable damage to the heart and lungs. Once again, the lack of internal hemorrhaging indicated these injuries had been sustained after death. Based on the nature of the injuries, Stormo concluded Blatz's body had probably been struck by the prop of a large water craft.[50]

Two days later, a toxicology test revealed Blatz's urine registered a blood alcohol content (BAC) of .30, while his blood had a BAC of .20. Re-interviewed after the autopsy, Tony Elskamp said, although Blatz had consumed a twelve-pack of beer and two bloody Mary's prior to bar hopping, the drowning victim was "probably the most sober of the group."[51]

Based on the autopsy findings that "there was no evidence of foul play," the La Crosse Police Department "exceptionally cleared" Blatz's death as an accidental drowning. [52]

In Chapter One, a suspicious death was defined as one that, due to the age and/or health of the deceased, lacks an explanation other than the involvement of another party. As it relates to Blatz's death, an elevated intoxication level offers a plausible explanation for the drowning. The average of the deceased's s urine and blood alcohol tests totaled .25, over three times the legal limit to drive. Like any drug, alcohol affects different people in different ways. Blatz's mother told investigators that, while her son did drink, she did not believe he abused alcohol. If this statement was indeed true, Blatz may have had a low alcohol tolerance.[53]

Unfortunately, the hard-partying lifestyle sometimes results in un-explainable and bizarre behaviors. One study conducted by the *National Institute on Alcohol Abuse and Alcoholism* (NIAAA) noted U.S. binge drinking rates were the "highest among young adults ages 18 to 25." This "high prevalence of drinking in young adults is a serious public health concern because alcohol use by this age group often is associated with a wide variety of risky behaviors and various negative consequences. Many of these consequences are immediate and tragic "[54]

Another NIAAA study indicated post-college "cyber-millennials" tend to exercise more, eat right, and smoke less, but consume significantly more alcohol than other demographic groups. As such, the NIAAA asked physicians to "pay particular attention to younger patients, since they are the most likely to have an unhealthy relationship with alcohol."[55]

By most accounts, Charles Blatz was a person of good character who met his demise, in part, due to an over indulgence of alcohol. Still, the Blatz family apparently believed more than alcohol was involved. On September 17, 1999, nearly two years after Blatz's death, La Crosse police were summoned to Riverside Park by Charles' brother, Barry, and his mother, Henrietta. The family had retained the services of Penny Bell, who operated a canine recovery unit.[56]

, Bell, two assistants, and Hoover — a canine search dog — checked the Mississippi River along the shore of Riverside Park, approximately six blocks northwest of the last known location of Charles Blatz. The dog also searched the La Crosse Municipal Boat Harbor and Copeland Park, located about two-and-a-half miles from the Happenings Tap. They found "nothing of any value."[57]

Bad Things Happen in Threes

On October 5, two days after Blatz's body was recovered, nineteen-year-old Anthony "Tony" Skifton, with a case of beer in tow, left a La Crosse house at 2:30 a.m. Five-and-a-half hours earlier, Skifton, along with two friends, Lad Dolittle and Rolland Gerard, met up with Jamie Baker at 402 S. 7th Avenue. After drinking a few beers, the four men left for a party three blocks west at 502 S. 5th Avenue. An occupant of the flat, Allan Low, told investigators that Skifton, a young man known as a hard-partier, sometimes stumbled and fell after drinking heavily. On occasion, party-goers used markers to draw crude sayings on Skifton's body after he passed out.[58]

After downing several beers and some tequila, Skifton left the party at about 2:30 a.m. He retrieved a twenty-pack of cheap beer, exited the back door, and fell down a small hill in the backyard. According to a party attendee, Ryan Torgerson, the very intoxicated man mumbled, "Ouch that hurt," eventually stood upright, and explained he was "all-right." Skifton then walked north into an alley and through the parking lot of Morrison and Associates (an accounting firm).[59]

When he failed to report for work on Monday, Skifton's employer telephoned his mother, Diane, to inquire about his whereabouts. Diane then contacted Dan Marcou, a family relative, who worked as an investigator with the La Crosse Police Department.[60]

Five days later, Skifton's corpse was located in the Isle La Plume Slough along Swift Creek, about two miles downstream from Houska Park. An examination of Skifton's body at the St. Francis morgue showed no overt signs of foul play; however, the zipper of his trousers had been completely pulled down.[61]

Skifton's body was later taken to the Minnesota Regional Coroner's

Office in the Twin Cities. An autopsy was performed by Dr. Lindsey Thomas, who listed the cause of death as drowning and further noted that "acute alcohol intoxication" played a critical role in the UW — La Crosse student's demise. The report further noted Skifton's bladder was empty and his BAC was .23.[62]

Having read about the missing student's drowning death in the local newspaper, a delivery driver for the G. Heileman Brewing Company, Steven Hildahl, contacted investigators to report he had observed a man matching Skifton's description on October 5th at about 3 a.m. Hildahl became concerned when he saw an inebriated young man, about five-foot-eight with long hair, carrying a thirty-pack of beer west on Market Street. Hildahl initially believed the man may have taken the case of beer from his nearby delivery truck and watched as the man walked west on the dead-end street that led to a walkway entrance to Houska Park.[63]

A short time later, Hildahl observed another man operating a fast moving wheelchair in the middle of Market Street, about eighty feet behind the man toting the case of beer. It was unclear, though, if the occupant of the wheelchair was attempting to catch up to the man with the beer, or simply making his way to the park.[64]

Although the autopsy report seemed to suggest that an intoxicated Skifton fell into the Mississippi River while relieving himself, a report of suspicious activity in the area raised some concerns. Two-and-a-half hours after Skifton left the house party, Adam Smith told police he had contact with two men in their twenties, one of whom was bleeding from some type of head injury. According to Smith, the men offered him five dollars to drive them from Houska Park to the 900 block of La Crosse Street. When Smith returned to the park, a red vehicle parked in front of his car. A man in a black goatee approached Smith, who rolled down his driver's side window. "Are you a cop?" the man asked. When Smith replied he was not an officer, the man asked, "Do you want a blow job?" Smith replied, "Hell no," and the man walked away.[65]

At the time of Skifton's disappearance, Houska Park was an apparent gathering spot for gay men to engage in anonymous sex. Since the zipper on the deceased student's trousers was down, and suspicious men were spotted in the area, the circumstances led some community members to suspect foul play. Although Skifton likely traveled to the park to rendezvous and drink with others, it seems unusual that he would have an empty bladder, which lends credence to the theory that Skifton — unsteady on his feet — fell into the Mississippi River while relieving himself.

For those who believed the local police simply wrote-off a suspicious death as an accidental drowning, the connection between a police official and the Skifton family seems to debunk the conspiracy. "My family has to be dragged through this over and over again every time there's another drowning," said La Crosse Police Lieutenant Dan Marcou, the uncle and godfather of Anthony Skifton. "Then they have to hear people applaud when there is talk about there being a serial killer." Like other public officials, Marcou believed the only killer was alcohol.[66]

The mysterious circumstances surrounding the Blatz and Skifton deaths served as an X-factor — the unknown variable that detectives try so diligently to unearth and plug into an investigative equation. The creation of a solid timeline is difficult when victims blend into a crowd and when potential witnesses' memories are impaired by alcohol. As the twenty-first century emerged, however, technology would ultimately fill in some of these unknown gaps.

CHAPTER THREE
BOTTOMS UP

The drowning deaths of Charles Blatz and Anthony Skifton shined a bright light on La Crosse's hard-partying culture. Besides the college crowd, the city of 51,000 hosts twenty-two annual festivals, where 200,000 attendees pump six million dollars into the local economy.[67]

Nonetheless, one would suspect these alcohol attributed drowning deaths may cause revelers to develop certain safeguards, such as friends that leave together and return together. This type of bond requires a shared responsibility between friends and acquaintances.

By all accounts, Nathan Kapfer, a member of the Viterbo College baseball team, was a good student. Those who knew Kapfer described the nineteen-year-old as "confident" and "cocky," but they also noted the Montana native had very few close friends. In fact, Kapfer's closest confidant appeared to be his live-in girlfriend, Angie Truttman.[68]

On Saturday, February 21, 1998, after Truttman left La Crosse for the weekend, Kapfer attended baseball practice from about 1 – 4 pm. Two hours later, "Nate," as he was known to those on campus, arrived at 207 S. 9th Street, the home of Kevin McDermott, who was hosting a team party. During the next five hours, Kapfer drank beer and assumed the role of a makeshift DJ. He left the party at about 11 p.m. and meandered downtown alone.[69]

At about midnight, Ryan Goodno ran into his fellow classmate, Kapfer, at The Library bar, located at 123 3rd Street. Goodno and Kapfer bought each other shots and talked for about twenty minutes. During the ensuing conversation, Goodno noticed Nate appeared "pretty intoxicated." A short time thereafter, Kapfer left to get a drink but never returned.[70]

At about 1:30 a.m., Kapfer appeared at Brother's Pub, about two blocks south of The Library bar, where he appeared "rather intoxicated." When asked for an ID, Kapfer produced a Viterbo school identification card with the name and likeness of "Rodney Hjorts." As he entered the bar, Kapfer was unsteady on his feet and bumped into a railing. Fifteen minutes later, two of the pub's employees, Josh Alresch and Kelly Slen-kowski, attempted to escort Nate to the door. As he was about to exit, the inebriated Kapfer stood at the exit's threshold and held the door open. Bouncer Christopher Kaufmann quickly approached and instructed him to let go of the door. Kapfer then shouted, "Fuck you." The verbal assault continued when Nate" yelled, "You're a piece of shit," and repeatedly gave Kaufmann "the finger." Standing in front of a large window, Kap-fer pulled down his pants, held his testicles in one hand, and screamed, "Right here, buddy!"[71]

A few seconds later, officers from the La Crosse Police Department arrived on the scene. During the investigation into the disturbance, Kap-fer volunteered to take a portable breath test (PBT), which registered a BAC of .077, a level below the legal limit to drive. The officers placed the student into a squad car and drove to 2nd and Pearl Streets, where Kapfer was issued citations for being in a tavern underage, possessing false identi-fication, and two counts of disorderly conduct. After being released, Kap-fer walked east and struck up a conversation with acquaintances, Stephen Fair, Jeremy Stock and Saad Samuel near 3rd and Pearl Streets. He did not, however, discuss the police contact. Kapfer then walked north by himself on 3rd Street.[72]

The following morning at 11 a.m., members of the Viterbo baseball team appeared at the La Crosse Police Department and reported that Kapfer had not returned home. A missing person/attempt to locate re-port was taken and a teletype was sent to other law enforcement agen-cies.[73]

On Monday morning, several members of the Viterbo baseball team searched the downtown area on foot. At around 9 a.m., Luke Hoff saw some paperwork oddly placed near the "Big Indian," a statue located on the west deck of the La Crosse Queen Gift Shop — a facility located at the north end of Riverside Park. After scaling a small fence, Hoff ob-served Kapfer's wallet, car keys, and the four municipal ordinance cita-tions, which were neatly placed at the base of the statute. A sergeant and an officer soon arrived, thoroughly searched the area, and observed no signs of a struggle. The fire department dragged the Mississippi River area adjacent to Riverside Park, but found no signs of the missing student.[74]

Once the La Crosse Police Department disseminated a missing per-sons alert to the local media, three reports of men matching Kapfer's description materialized. On Sunday, February 22, at about 6 a.m., Lawrence Todd had purchased a newspaper at a Kwik Trip gas station near Rose and Logan Streets, about two-and-half-miles north of Riverside Park. A young white male wearing a Viterbo baseball cap struck up a conversation with Todd as the two walked south on Rose Street. The man had "alcohol on his breath" and was unsteady on his feet. A short time later, the man in the ball cap, who Todd said appeared to match Kapfer's description, entered a Hardee's restaurant.[75]

On February 24, between five and six a.m., Mike Bahr, an employee of Market & Johnson, arrived at a parking ramp construction site near 4th and Jay Streets. A young man exited the heated basement of the structure and walked north on 5th Street. Although the man appeared to match Kapfer's description, and the ramp was just blocks from where he was last seen, two full days had passed. It was unlikely the man was Kapfer.[76]

Another possible witness, Carl Schoenfeld, saw a young man standing on the La Crosse River Bridge on N. 3rd Street on February 22 at about 1 a.m. The man, who was wearing a green shirt, "seemed oblivious to the rest of the world around him" as he stared at the water below. However, if the time of sighting was correct, Schoenfeld had observed the man thirty minutes prior to Kapfer exposing himself outside of Brother's Pub.[77]

Then, on April 4, forty days after the Viterbo student's wallet and car keys were found outside the Riverside Park gift ship, a boater contacted the La Crosse Fire Department concerning a body floating in the water near Running Slough, about four miles to the south of Riverside Park. The corpse, along with other debris, was hung up on a snag, and the head and upper body protruded from the water. As is the case with many drowning victims, gas had caused the corpse to bloat and come to the surface. Based on the clothing description and jewelry, the deceased was identified as Nathan Kapfer.[78]

Three days later, an autopsy was performed by Dr. Lindsey Thomas at a regional medical facility in Hastings, Minnesota. The only injuries Kapfer had sustained were two small bruises along his left leg — consistent with bumping into an object. A toxicology screen indicated Kapfer's BAC was .22, almost three times the legal limit to drive. The cause of death was drowning by undermined means. No evidence of foul play was detected during the autopsy and the La Crosse Police Department "exceptionally cleared" the death investigation.[79]

Nonetheless, the death of Nathan Kapfer is fodder for armchair cops — members of the laity who have never worked in a law enforcement capacity. After all, the police had the intoxicated man in the back of their squad car. In hindsight, armchair cops could argue the officers should have given Kapfer a ride or, based on the indecent exposure complaint, taken the student to jail. On the other hand, La Crosse police officers patrol the downtown entertainment district every weekend, and undoubtedly have had contact with hundreds, if not thousands, of drunken young men. If these officers effected custodial arrests for every alcohol related disturbance, very few officers would be available to keep the peace at bar closing time.

As it relates to the decision to catch and release Kapfer, the result of the portable breath test (.077 BAC) may have led Officer Secord to conclude the underage drinker had a low alcohol tolerance. In Wisconsin, a PBT result can be used to formulate probable cause to cite or arrest; however, the results are not admissible in court as prima facie evidence. PBT machines are sometimes impacted by the weather. In cooler temperatures, "it is possible for the moisture in the breath to condense onto the airway surface of the tester, and cause alcohol present to condense with it." As a result, a reading can appear significantly lower and/or future tests can be affected.[80]

Some specialists believe the horizontal gaze nystagmus (HGN) field test is the most accurate for detecting the presence of blood alcohol. HGN is "an involuntary, repetitive eye movement. The eye appears to quickly bounce back and forth over a short extent." The presence of alcohol in the body impacts "the angle of gaze at which nystagmus is first observed." No equipment is required for this test and courts have considered HGN results reliable for probable cause determinations. In Kapfer's case, it appears the HGN test was not administered, although it is unclear if the officers on the scene that morning were trained to administer the HGN field test.[81]

Another issue that affects an officer's decision in the field is the availability of a twenty-four hour detoxification facility. Dane County is one of the few governmental entities in Wisconsin with such a center. If an officer on the street has contact with an individual incapacitated by alcohol, the officer can take an impaired person into custody vis-à-vis an emergency detention. If such a facility had existed in La Crosse, Kapfer would have been a prime candidate.

Still, similar to the Blatz family, Kapfer's relatives appeared to suspect more than just alcohol. On July 30, 1999, seven months after their son had disappeared, Nathan's father, Mark, retained the services of Doris "Penny" Bell and her canine, Hoover. The search began at 7 a.m. in Riverside Park. Bell reported the dog "made several hits on the floating barge" moored at the park and also hit on the area surrounding the Big Indian statute. The dog then tracked eastbound and hit on an old railroad bridge. Hoover proceeded to walk about one hundred yards and "began to weave from side-to-side" before coming to a stop. Bell told an officer the dog's behavior signaled Kapfer had entered a vehicle that then drove away. The canine allegedly located Kapfer's scent at several downtown taverns; however, investigators were skeptical.[82]

Lieutenant Brohmer noted the dog had allegedly hit on a few areas previously marked with spray paint — the same paint sometimes used at crime scenes. Moreover, the path Hoover hit on was not a paved road but rather a railroad bed, which, at the time of Kapfer's disappearance, was covered with snow. Consequently, the path would have been "very difficult to traverse with a vehicle."[83]

In an effort to check the veracity of Bell's canine hits, Brohmer contacted Pat Moffit, a bloodhound handler with the Sonoma County, California, Sheriff's Department. After being briefed on the La Crosse canine search, Moffit reported that dog searches in an urban setting, where the pavement is subjected to heat and rain, as well as foot and vehicle traffic, "would be difficult a short time after the incident, let alone" months after the fact.[84]

Similar to the Blatz investigation, an elevated intoxication level offers a plausible explanation for the drowning death of Kapfer. Unlike Blatz, however, Kapfer had engaged in some rather bizarre behavior when he exposed himself outside of Brother's Pub. Members of the Viterbo baseball team told investigators that Kapfer's conduct was out of character. Kapfer's girlfriend, Angie Truttman, told investigators she "worried a lot" because Nate "did not want to disappoint his parents." The neat placement of Kapfer's wallet and car keys near the Big Indian strongly suggests the intoxicated student was despondent from receiving the four citations.[85]

Reckless Abandon

Jeffrey Geesey was a young man who grappled with addiction. Just prior to his twentieth birthday, the UW — La Crosse student was convicted of operating a motor vehicle while intoxicated for a third time. According to Geesey's mother, Laurie, her son began drinking at age fifteen. Jeffrey's refusal to address his addiction caused a rift between his parents.[86]

Those closest to Geesey believed he was a ticking time bomb — a classic alcoholic traversing a tortuous, self-destructive path until implosion. A new term has emerged for persons with reckless lifestyles — autoassassination. In other words, the bad choices some people make play a significant role in their premature deaths.

On April 15, 1999, after Geesey's parents learned their son had not been seen for five days, the student's parents contacted the University of Wisconsin – La Crosse Protective Services division. When Jeffrey's roommate, Jay Heal, and a Sanford Hall resident assistant said they had not observed Jeffrey since April 10, Richard Geesey contacted the La Crosse Police Department.[87]

Almost immediately, an officer interviewed Geesey's friend, Leah Berard, who initially said Geesey had been at her Vine Street apartment on April 10, but left around 9 p.m. to go drinking. Four days later, Laurie Geesey contacted the police to report that Berard had "withheld information" concerning her son's whereabouts.[88]

When re-interviewed, Berard admitted providing false information because she feared being cited for underage drinking. Investigators learned Geesey had met a group of friends at Berard's apartment on April 10 at around 9 p.m. The group, which included Berard, her father Nick, Julie Seramur, Brian Hager and Sean Glavich, walked to Big Al's tavern, located in the 100 block of S. 3rd Street, where they were joined by Seth Zondag. The group drank at Big Al's for about two hours, then walked to the Bodega Brew Pub, a block west on S. 4th Street.[89]

At 11:45 p.m., Berard, her father, and Seramur left the brew pub and returned to her apartment. The remainder of the group walked to Bronco Billy's tavern, then to Club Millennium, located at 121 S. 3rd Street. Two of the men present with Geesey, Sean Glavich, and Brian Hagar, told investigators they were so intoxicated they did not recall much after leaving the brew pub. However, Seth Zondag, who was the least intoxicated, said Geesey began chatting with a petite white female with brown hair. When Glavich and Hagar began to feel sick, Zondag decided to leave with the two men. Geesey, who was "pretty intoxicated" and intent on chatting with the woman, stayed behind. As he left Club Millennium, Zondag observed there were about thirty-five people inside, but Geesey was the only white male.[90]

Since the white female chatting with Geesey was the last known person to speak with the missing student, La Crosse police focused on identifying the woman. One of the bartenders on duty at the club in the early morning hours of April 11, Dawn Van Geertruy, recalled seeing a group of "college aged guys." She remembered the young men because they had ordered a pitcher of beer, which was unusual for club patrons. She further recalled that several Native Americans were in the bar that morning and they also drank pitchers of beer.[91]

The other Club Millennium bartender, Nichole Loken, recalled three or four college-aged white males at the bar. The males performed some "magic tricks" for her and she "was very sure" one of them was the missing student. However, Loken did not recall Geesey speaking to any females and did not know any female patrons who matched the description provided by Zondag.[92]

On April 25, Doris "Penny" Bell and Hoover returned to La Crosse. Hoover hit on the entry door to the apartments above Club Millennium. The exterior door to the apartments units is inaccessible without a key and none of the occupants recalled seeing Geesey. Local cab companies were also contacted, but none reported having any passengers who matched the missing student's description.[93]

In the interim, some false sightings of Geesey were reported. Detectives also probed and seemingly debunked an anonymous tip the missing student was killed by a man from Minneapolis, who had struck "a white dude" over the head with a beer bottle.[94]

On the morning of May 22, two fisherman caught a glimpse of a body floating in the water in Running Slough, just east of the 7th Street boat landing. An officer from Shelby Police Department and two firefighters pulled the corpse, which matched the clothing description of Geesey, from the water.[95]

Two days later, the body was transported to the Regional Medical Center in Hastings, Minnesota, where an autopsy was performed by Dr. Lindsey Thomas. A bogus ID card Geesey used to gain entry into taverns, under the name "Terry Burgin," and a health insurance card bearing Geesey's name, were found on the body. Dental records supplied by Geesey's parents positively identified the body.[96]

An external and internal examination of Geesey's body showed no signs of trauma, although an abrasion to the stomach from "aquatic feeding" was found on the body. Toxicology results indicated the deceased's BAC was .42, over five times the legal limit to drive. The post-mortem state of the brain stem was "consistent with that of a drowning victim." An unofficial report noted Geesey had previously sustained "four shallow, self-inflicted scars on his arms," which emanated from a prior cutting incident that required hospitalization.[97]

On the same day as the autopsy, La Crosse police were contacted by Jerry Erickson, who said he had observed a Nike three-quarter high athletic shoe along the south bank of the Mississippi River near the "gravel pit" — an area located about a mile north of the Running Slough. Like the others who had entered the river and drowned, Geesey's body was swept south by the fast moving current.[98]

Although a break in the investigative timeline exists, and the young woman last seen chatting with the deceased was never identified, the La Crosse Police Department — based on the totality of the circumstances — determined Geesey's death was an accidental drowning. This conclusion was reached, in part, due to Geesey's prior self-inflicted cutting, which investigators apparently believed was a suicide attempt. The highly intoxicated Geesey was also concerned about a pending court case. As was the case with the Blatz and Kapfer incidents, family members suspected more than alcohol intoxication. "Someone is doing this," said Richard Geesey.[99]

Almost two years later, another young man went missing after leaving a tavern. This time, however, witnesses were able to confirm he left alone.

On March 2, 2001, Ethel Runingen contacted the West Salem Police Department to report her twenty-three-year-old son, Patrick, missing. Ethel told officers her son had left home the previous night, did not return, and failed to report for work in the morning. The West Salem PD learned Patrick had taken a cab from his home at 126 ½ Leonard Street at about 9:30 p.m., and traveled ten miles to the Nutbush City Limits, a tavern on the far north side of La Crosse.[100]

West Salem police made contact with Michelle Nauman, a bartender at the tavern, who recalled Runingen sitting at the end of the bar by himself. Although she did not remember serving him, Runingen did ask Nauman to call him a cab. Busy and working the bar by herself, Nauman tossed the customer a quarter to use a pay telephone. After placing a call, Runingen returned to his seat. When a cab arrived, the bartender turned to notify Runingen, but he was gone.[101]

Officers from area police departments searched the banks of the Black River, a body of water just four blocks east of the tavern, but found no signs of the missing man. When the *La Crosse Tribune* published an article concerning Runingen's disappearance, witnesses began contacting West Salem police.

Barb Kaiser told investigators she stopped by the Nutbush City Limits with a few friends on March 1. Between 11 p.m. – midnight, she observed Runingen leaving the bar "very intoxicated." Kaiser and her friends remarked that they hoped the young man was not driving. Kaiser watched as he walked south toward La Crosse.[102]

On March 7, Troy Holzer called the West Salem police and provided a critical detail. On the morning of Runingen's disappearance, Holzer and two other friends drove to the Black River beach near the Onalaska Spillway. The would-be fishermen noticed an "unusual hole in the ice not too far from shore." They returned to the area around 3 p.m. and put a boat in the water. While en route to the unusual hole, the boat broke through the quarter-inch ice. Once there, the men observed a black stocking cap and a pack of Marlboro Lite 100 cigarettes "floating in the hole." Before leaving, the men plucked the floating objects from the water and secured them in their boat.[103]

Holzer told investigators that the hole in the ice was approximately thirty feet from shore, near Camp 22 on Fisherman's Road. This location is on the opposite side of the Black River at the Nutbush City Limits. On March 8, at about 10:15 a.m., Holzer pointed out the area of the now-melted hole in the ice to firefighters. Within a few minutes of dragging the river, Runingen's body was recovered.[104]

The following day, Dr. Eric Burton performed Runingen's autopsy. The only trauma to the body were two scrapes on the thighs. Burton theorized the marks were likely caused when Runingen made a last ditch effort to push himself from the frigid water and onto the ice. The foam found in the deceased's airway and lungs is consistent with fresh water drowning. Toxicology tests listed Runingen's BAC at .24, which meant he had consumed alcohol for some time prior to his arrival at the Nutbush City Limits. The cause of death was listed as drowning with "alcohol as a contributing factor."[105]

Contrary to the prior drowning deaths, witness statements enabled investigators to create a solid investigative timeline. Runingen had left the bar alone and the fishermen's discovery of the hole in the ice made it possible to trace the missing man's staggered path across the Black River towards French Island.

CHAPTER FOUR

NOTHING GOOD HAPPENS
ON A HALF MOON

At a recent get-together, I spoke with an individual who believed a serial killer was responsible for the drowning deaths of young men in La Crosse. "Why is it," this person asked, "that there are college towns all over Wisconsin but these drownings only happen in La Crosse?" The early batch of reports emanating from La Crosse had, unfortunately, skewed this individual's perception of events. The drowning deaths of young men in the Badger State have occurred in several other cities.

One such locale is Eau Claire, a college town located in the northwestern part of the state. The Chippewa River cuts a wide swath through the campus of the University of Wisconsin — Eau Claire. A cement footbridge allows students to cross the river from the lower campus and travel north to the Hass Fine Arts Center and Water Street. On Friday and Saturday nights, students flock to the Water Street District — a three block stretch of taverns, restaurants, and small businesses. The Chippewa River flows directly to the south of Water Street. If one would prefer, a bike path directly west of the foot bridge follows the river to a strip mall and a fitness center with fast food restaurants. The path continues, and, a block later, reaches The Pickle, a tavern that advertises weekly drink specials.

The city's namesake, the Eau Claire River, flows into the Chippewa River at their confluence downtown. This area is easily accessible to campus via a foot bridge and a transformed railroad trestle, which crosses the river and ends at the entrance to Phoenix Park. A slew of restaurants and pubs are located between Wisconsin and Madison Streets, less than two blocks north of the old railroad bridge.

Students who were freshmen at UW – Eau Claire in 2002 were only middle schoolers when Richard Hlavaty, Charles Blatz and Anthony Skifton perished, and high school sophomores when Jeffrey Geesey drowned. That passage of time apparently impacted the memories of those at greatest risk — young men abandoned by their friends after heavy bouts of drinking.

Those closest to twenty-three-year-old Craig Burrows saw red flags everywhere. On September 28, at 5:30 a.m., Burrows was released from the Eau Claire County Jail after completing a four-day sentence for driving under the influence.[106]

At about 8:30 p.m., Burrows and a friend, Travis Loftgren, arrived at the Brat Kabin, located in the 300 block of Water Street. The bar's manager, Brian Schwechel, knew Burrows as a "frequent" patron who "drinks a lot." On at least one prior occasion, Burrows was so intoxicated that Schwechel stopped serving him. According to Loftgren, his friend seemed to be in a "good mood" and was "very intoxicated." Between midnight and 12:30 a.m., Burrows began dancing with a young woman. Another friend, Olie Wold, also saw Burrows dancing, but at around closing time, realized he had suddenly disappeared. Wold speculated Burrows left for another bar.[107]

A day and a half later, Burrows' brother, Todd, contacted the Eau Claire Police Department to report Craig had not returned home and no one had seen him since 1 a.m. on September 29. He described his brother as being almost six feet tall and weighing a lean one-hundred-and-fifty pounds. Friends said Craig Burrows was last seen wearing a brown sweater with blue stripes, a white t-shirt, and blue jeans. The missing man was known to be " a heavy drinker."[108]

Burrows' mother, Chris Fenner, told investigators her son had attended counseling after his father's death, but "quit going to the sessions." She further explained Craig was aware he had a drinking problem, but "felt he could control it."[109]

Over a week passed before forty-four-year-old John Bachmeier parked his green Pontiac Grand Am in the upper lot near the Half Moon Park. When he walked to the beach area, Bachmeier saw an "obviously deceased" person floating in the water to the east of the sand beach swimming area. He ran to his car and drove to the Eau Claire Police Department.[110]

Bachmeier returned to the park with a police lieutenant. Approximately ten feet from shore, they observed the body of a male with blonde hair, floating face down in the water. The male's clothing matched that of Craig Burrows. A fire department rescue unit was summoned to the scene and recovered the body.[111]

An officer with a video camera documented the position and recovery of the corpse, which could been seen about thirty feet to the southeast of the boat landing. Members of the Eau Claire Fire Department also deployed an underwater camera to determine if the deceased had suffered any trauma. Near the shoreline, fire personnel turned the body over and officers recognized the decedent as Craig Burrows. Five crushed Miller Lite cans, found five feet west of the boat landing, were also photographed and recovered. It was unclear if they were relevant to the investigation.[112]

An ambulance was summoned to the scene and the body was taken to Sacred Heart Hospital in Eau Claire, where Medical Examiner John Folstad conducted an external examination. The body was free of ligature marks and had sustained no observable external trauma. A pack of sugar-free gum and seven dollars was found inside Burrows' right front pants pocket. The front portion of the decedent's pants contained a "large amount of mud," which likely emanated from the body's post mortem resting spot at the lake bottom. A wallet found on the floating corpse contained several items that identified the owner as Burrows.[113]

The following day, an autopsy was conducted by Dr. Thomas Hadley, a pathologist at the hospital. The skin on Burrows' head, neck, and upper chest showed signs of post mortem lividity. When coupled with the mud on the front of the pants, the patterns of lividity appeared consistent with the body being found face down in the water, where accumulated gases later brought the corpse to the surface. An internal examination of the cranium showed no signs of trauma. Based on this examination, Hadley listed the cause of death as drowning. A toxicology report from the Wisconsin State Laboratory of Hygiene indicated Burrows' BAC was .26, over three times the legal limit to drive.[114]

At the time of his death, Burrows resided at 928 Walnut Street, just over two miles north of the Brat Kabin. With only seven dollars on his person, he may have decided to travel home from Water Street on foot instead of summoning a cab. Traveling on foot, Burrows' most likely route was north on Fifth Street and west on Randall Street — a path leading directly to Half Moon Park.

Based on the totality of the circumstances — a high level of intoxication, no signs of trauma to the body, and the lake located on the route home — the Eau Claire Police Department cleared Burrows' death as an apparent accidental drowning. As was the case with Jeffrey Geesey, Burrows was a very intoxicated young man with a drinking problem who was last seen in the company of an unknown female at a tavern.

Grassy Knoll Conspiracies

Most conspiracy theories incorporate enough strands of truth or are given life through a series of coincidences. Just six weeks after Craig Burrows' body was pulled from Half Moon Lake, four young adults — three in Minnesota and one in Eau Claire — went missing. Two of the four incidents poured fuel onto the fire of a budding serial killer hypothesis.

On October 30, 2002, twenty-one-year-old Erika Dahlquist was last seen leaving a Brainerd, Minnesota, bar in the company of a man, later identified as William Gene Myears. Although investigators had a solid suspect, and Dahlquist was presumed to be deceased, searchers were unable to locate her body.[115]

The following evening, University of Minnesota student Christopher Jenkins and a group of friends left a keg party and traveled to the Lone Tree Bar & Grill, located in Minneapolis' warehouse district. At around midnight, two off-duty police officers moonlighting as bouncers removed Jenkins — clad in an American Indian Halloween costume — from the premise. Jenkins' jacket, which included his keys, wallet and cellular telephone, remained behind inside the tavern. Searchers looked for the missing student but came up empty handed.[116]

Then, on November 7, Jeffrey Noll contacted the Eau Claire Police Department to report his son, Michael, had failed to return home after "going to the bars last night." Michael's college roommates, Adam Wood and Michael Lauenstein, told police they had gone out the night before to celebrate Noll's birthday. They last observed their roommate on November 6, at 11:30 p.m. at the Nasty Habit, a Water Street tavern. Noll was intoxicated and was asked to leave by a barroom bouncer.[117]

Officers canvassed the Water Street business district for possible witnesses and searched the banks of the nearby Chippewa River. The assistant bar manager of the Nasty Habit, Lawrence Leonard, said an already intoxicated Noll arrived at the bar around 10 p.m. in the company of six other friends. On a scale of one to ten, with ten being intoxicated to the point of passing out, Leonard listed Noll as an eight. Twenty minutes later, Noll approached a "heavier set" man from behind and grabbed his buttocks. After the heavier set man left the tavern without incident, Leonard instructed a bouncer to ask Noll to leave the premise.[118]

Then, on the evening of November 10, an undergraduate student at St. John's University in Collegeville, Minnesota, was reported missing. The preceding evening, Joshua Guimond left a party at about 11 p.m. to use the bathroom. When he failed to return, his friends assumed he had walked back to his campus apartment at the Saint Maur House. The following day, after Guimond missed a scheduled "mock trial meeting," his car was found undisturbed in its usual parking spot.[119]

Deputies from the Stearns County Sheriff's Department, campus Life Safety officers, and two dozen volunteers, searched residence halls and vacant rooms. A helicopter with infrared technology was summoned to search the St. John's University campus. A "trained bloodhound" followed Guimond's scent to a channel on Stumpf Lake, less than a half mile from campus. An extensive land and water search was conducted, but it appeared the promising business student had simply fallen off the face of the earth.[120]

A week later, some members of the St. John's University community feared the worst. Reverend Paul Fitt, a faculty resident, suspected foul play. "I'm curious to find out whether these three or four cases in state are related," Fitt told reporter Nick Watts. "I hope it's not an abduction, because that would not give closure to the parents. They've just dragged through two lakes again, they've found nothing — where else could he be?"[121]

Back in Eau Claire, police began retracing Noll's whereabouts. An officer interviewed Molly Seavers, who saw the missing student and at least three of his friends at Mogie's Pub on Water Street at 8:30 p.m., two hours prior to Noll being asked to leave the Nasty Habit. Seavers said Noll was "intoxicated when she saw him."[122]

Police also identified the heavier set man groped by Noll as Jeffrey Holz. After leaving the Nasty Habit, Holz watched as the intoxicated student crossed Water Street, moved through the parking lot of the M&I Bank, then walked east down an alley.[123]

On November 11, a break came in the investigation. After reading a report of Noll's disappearance in the newspaper, eighty-year-old Harriet Anderson recalled an incident at her home. She contacted the Eau Claire Police Department, located directly across the street. On November 6, at about 11:30 p.m., the elderly woman heard "a noise" outside her residence. When she opened the rear door, a highly intoxicated white male, wearing a white Minnesota Gophers ball cap, "pushed his way into her home."[124]

As the young man staggered inside her living room, Anderson was able to "convince" the intruder he was at the wrong house. The man glanced around Anderson's residence, dropped his ball cap, and exited the rear door. He then walked directly to the front of the house, was unable to open the locked door, and left the area.[125]

Anderson described the twenty-something young man as five-foot-eight, slender, and "very pale," with a strong odor of alcoholic beverages "coming from his person." The elderly woman believed the Minnesota Gophers cap was Noll's. She further told investigators the picture of the missing man in the newspaper strongly resembled the drunken trespasser.[126]

After speaking with Anderson, the Eau Claire Police Department informed the press Noll was last observed a block away from police headquarters. The news release further noted that search dogs and officers were in the process of canvassing the area. Residents living within a ten block radius of Anderson's abode were asked to check their basements and spare rooms for the missing man.[127]

While living in Eau Claire, Noll, a Rochester, Minnesota native, resided at 1020 First Avenue, directly west of the Chippewa River. Based on his last easterly direction of travel in the alley, investigators theorized he traveled north on Third Street to Grand Avenue and east to Oxford Street, just three-tenths of a mile south of his residence. As such, the search for the missing student focused on the closest body of water — the Chippewa River.[128]

With Michael Noll in the wind, investigators received reports of mistaken or false sightings, as well as calls from grassy knoll conspiracy-type theorists. A reporter for the *Eau Claire Leader-Telegram*, Christina O'Brien, told police an anonymous party had telephoned the newspaper and claimed she had observed Noll at a local restaurant. In an effort to identify the caller, a detective obtained a subpoena for telephone records. When the subpoena was returned, a detective interviewed Bobbie Zebro, who said that on November 9 she saw a man matching Noll's description in a vehicle being serviced at the drive-thru window at a Chippewa Falls Burger King. Zebro said the man she believed might be Noll was the driver and was wearing a white ball cap with "some sort of symbol on the front."[129]

On November 19, an *Associated Press* report regarding Noll's disappearance appeared in the *Wisconsin State Journal* with the byline "UW-Eau Claire student among four missing." Although the article contained little additional information, the reach of the statewide paper generated a slew of tips from armchair sleuths.[130]

One woman, who asked to remain anonymous, emailed the Eau Claire Police Department to offer a possible theory. Four months prior to Noll's disappearance, the woman's boyfriend, a man in town from Atlanta, visited the Pioneer Tavern on Water Street. When he failed to return to his girlfriend's apartment until the following morning, the man explained that an unknown woman had bought him a drink. Twelve hours later, he allegedly awoke on a city beach, and had no memory of how he got there. "This may be the reason that males are disappearing from bars," wrote the woman, "especially males who don't drink often and do things that they normally wouldn't do." Cynics, such as myself, would also chalk-up the boyfriend's sudden memory loss to a woman, but for more typical reasons.[131]

Another possible theory came in the form of a letter to the Eau Claire Police Department from George Reykdal, who resided near the UW — Eau Claire campus for a number of years. The tipster noted he had "read the papers with interest regarding the Michael Noll case and the three students in Minnesota, who similarly went missing. Police have stated that they don't think the four cases are connected. I would speculate otherwise." However, instead of scrutinizing the activities of the missing students, the armchair detective based his entire premise on the episode of *Criminal Minds* dedicated to comparative investigative analysis.[132]

Reykdal offered three points to support his theory. He argued "three of the four cases happened in college towns"; that "three of the four cases happened in college towns with prominent bodies of water"; and, finally, in "three of the four cases, intoxicated students went missing in the early morning hours." Absent a description of possible suspects — save the Dahlquist investigation — Reykdal wrote, "I think what you have, possibly, is a thrill-kill group of low-life twenty-something males, who prey on sidewalks in the early morning hours" Noting he had previously been "cased by a carload of thugs" while residing in Eau Claire, Reykdal advanced a theory that the bodies of water were part of the killing ritual, where the suspects "sweep the victims from the sidewalk and throw them into a body of water to drown."[133]

There are, of course, several problems with Reykdal's hypothesis. Sweeping a person from the sidewalk would likely result in a struggle that would require the use of ligatures to secure the victim. The Minnesota-based *Center for Homicide Research* defines "thrill killings" as "long drawn-out killing processes that include bondage, strangulation, sexual activity, and physical torture of a victim who is alive and 'aware of what is happening' and able to feel pain." If force was used during the abduction, trauma would be observed during an autopsy. Moreover, even a highly intoxicated person would likely scream for help — cries that would be heard by witnesses in the middle of the night.[134]

Another tipster contacted the Eau Claire Police Department to report that a young man, Colin Cayce, had accepted a ride from a stranger after a night of drinking in Eau Claire. The caller said Cayce awoke the following morning in "someone's yard and had a black eye."[135]

An investigator located Cayce, who said the incident had occurred in Menomonie, Wisconsin, near 12th and Broadway Streets in the later part of August or early September. Just after midnight, Cayce, who was very intoxicated, left a drinking party and was walking home when a white male in an SUV stopped at the curb. The driver asked Cayce if he would like a ride so "he wouldn't get picked up by the police." Cayce entered the SUV, but soon asked the driver to pull to the curb so he could vomit. The driver also exited the SUV and offered his intoxicated passenger oral sex. Cayce believed he had simply walked away and passed out in a park. When he awoke, Cayce had a swollen lip and a scratch on his right eye. Cayce, however, told detectives he sometimes imagines things during heavy bouts of drinking and was unsure if the incident actually occurred.[136]

Two days later, another conspiracy emerged. An Eau Claire police officer was approached in the lobby of the city's law enforcement center by twenty-year-old Melissa O'Brien, who claimed a man with connections to *La Cosa Nostra*, Thomas Antinucci, knew where Michael Noll's body was buried.[137]

According to O'Brien, Antinucci explained he had followed Noll from Water Street to an elderly woman's residence. When the intoxicated student noticed the alleged mobster following him, Noll explained he was stopping by his grandmother's house. When the two men entered the home, an elderly woman ordered them to leave. Antinucci warned the woman she better "not say a word about them being there," and told O'Brien "he had made a mistake not taking Noll's hat when he dropped it."[138]

The purported Mafioso further told O'Brien investigators would not find Noll's body in the Chippewa River, but said the missing student's body was buried nearby. Antinucci offered to show O'Brien the shallow grave, but she refused to visit the alleged burial site. O'Brien also told investigators Antinucci admitted killing Craig Burrows, and placed the deceased man's corpse in Half Moon Lake because "he had nowhere else to put the body at the time."[139]

Investigators soon learned Thomas Antinucci was an alias for Thomas James Amort, a twenty-five-year-old white male with an outstanding felony warrant for burglary. The Eau Claire Police Department disseminated a wanted flier for Amort that described the alleged member of the underworld as being five-foot-five and weighing two hundred pounds.[140]

Forty-eight hours later, two patrol officers located Amort and placed him under arrest for the felony warrant. When interrogated at the Eau Claire County Jail, Amort told detectives he had previously met the missing student at the Nasty Habit bar, but had fabricated his mob connections, as well as the information pertaining to Noll and Burrows, to impress and hopefully date Melissa O'Brien.[141]

On November 26, twenty days after Noll's disappearance, Eau Claire Police Department Deputy Chief Gary Foster suspended the search for the missing student. "We may try dogs on the river again," Foster wrote in a memo. "However, that will be up to the handlers. The river was scanned by sonar in areas where it was feasible without success. Any and all leads will continue to be followed as they come in."[142]

Nonetheless, the Noll family, desperate for answers, retained the services of psychic Taylor "Sammy" Graham, who agreed to pass along "her visions" to investigators. Graham related she had a vision of Noll leaving a celebration after consuming alcohol. A car pulled alongside the student, who leaned into the car to provide directions to the driver. The automobile was "an older vintage vehicle with lots of chrome — something unusual about the license plate, perhaps a Buick or Oldsmobile." Graham then claimed Noll died from two blows — one to the head and another to the chest — and his body was lying on concrete in a building slated for demolition. The psychic further stated Noll's murder was premeditated, the suspect wanted to get caught, and the killer suffered from a "homosexual" identity crisis.[143]

To bolster her creditability, Graham told an investigator she had solved "a baby murder" in Waterford, Connecticut, in the 1980s, where she worked with a detective named Steve Davis. When an Eau Claire investigator called the Waterford Police Department, he was told no one by the name of "Steve Davis" had been employed there. In another instance, "Sammy" claimed she had solved a homicide in Halfmoon Bay, California, but Police Sergeant Dave Bolster reported the psychic had "described a location specifically," which police "checked and no body was found."[144]

Another tip came from Noll's father, Jeffrey. Prior to Michael's disappearance, he told his father about some suspicions about a male teacher he met while fulfilling his student teaching requirements. The teacher had previously ran into the now missing student at the Pioneer Tavern and at some point invited him to a dinner.[145]

When a detective contacted the teacher, the man explained the dinner was offered by the school district for those with "teaching status." The teacher also said he did have contact with Noll at the Pioneer Tavern after participating in a volleyball match across the street. According to a police report, the teacher had a "contact history" with the Eau Claire Police Department that suggested he was gay. When asked about his sexual orientation, the teacher "seemed intimidated by the question" and "declined answering that question."[146]

Just before Christmas, another would-be psychic contacted the police. Janet L. Fitzgerald had a "sense" Noll's body was located in the Eau Claire River under the Barstow Street Bridge, just two blocks east of its confluence with the Chippewa River. To ensure the case detective understood her directions, Fitzgerald drew a map with an arrow purportedly showing where the missing student's body could be found. Although a sonar scan of the area had previously been conducted, police checked the banks of the much smaller Eau Claire River but found no signs of Noll.[147]

Over the course of the next three months, the investigation of Noll's disappearance turned cold. On March 25, 2003, at about 5:30 p.m., Nathan and Bethany Walker were walking their dogs along the eastern coast line of Carson Park, a land mass that divides Half Moon Lake. As the couple approached the Birch Pavilion, they saw a body protruding through the ice. The couple quickly returned to their car, drove to the headquarters of the Eau Claire Police Department, and flagged down Officer Mark Pieper. The officer followed the Walkers back to Carson Park. Using a set of binoculars, Pieper could see "the head and left shoulder of a human jutting out of the ice" on Half Moon Lake, about sixty feet from shore.[148]

The officers secured the area until investigators and a fire department recovery team could respond. A boat was placed in the water and a detective accompanied the fire rescue team to the location of the body. After photographing and marking the scene, fire personnel used saws and other tools to perforate the ice and recover the corpse, which was placed face down on a wooden board and inserted into a large, orange body bag. Once on shore, a medical examiner found a wallet in the rear pants pocket. The wallet contained the identification of Michael Noll. Detectives noted the clothing on the body matched "the original video we had [from various drinking establishments] from the night that Mr. Noll disappeared." The body was conveyed to Sacred Heart Hospital and placed in a freezer.[149]

The following day, Noll's corpse was taken to the Ramsey County Medical Center in St. Paul, Minnesota. Dr. Michael McGee, who conducted the autopsy, determined the student had died from fresh water drowning and listed the manner of death as "accidental." McGee found no evidence of trauma or ligature marks on the body. A toxicology test indicated Noll's BAC was .202. A total of $12.25 was also recovered from the wallet.[150]

Although Noll's body was discovered closer to Carson Park than the Half Moon Lake boat launch, he probably walked west on Fulton Street, instead of east towards his residence, after leaving Harriet Anderson's Oxford Avenue home. This staggered path led Noll directly to Half Moon Lake.

In early November, the temperature of Half Moon Lake is about 50 degrees. Since the human body weighs more than water, individuals who lose consciousness in water sink to the bottom, unless obstructed by an object. As the deceased descends farther, the water pressure causes gases to congregate in the body's upper torso. The farther the body sinks, the less buoyant a corpse becomes. Eau Claire's mean temperature on the date Noll disappeared was 32 degrees. The cooler November water in Half Moon Lake, which averages six-feet in depth, likely prevented gases in Noll's body from forming quickly. As a result, his corpse remain submerged for "several weeks."[151]

By the time the bacterial action in Noll's body accelerated, he likely rose to the bottom of the ice formation and floated with the lake current. During the spring thaw, the accumulating gases pushed the corpse through the thin ice until it was observed by the Walkers.[152]

As one would expect, the location of the body and the results of the autopsy disproved the murder theories. Noll did not sustain two body blows, which again debunked the visions of purported psychic Taylor "Sammy" Graham. The lack of trauma and ligature marks discredited armchair sleuth George Reykdal's theory of rogue twenty-somethings perpetuating thrill-kills. Noll's body was found in Half Moon Lake and not in the Eau Claire River, therefore, marginalizing the "sense" of would-be psychic Janet L. Fitzgerald. The missing student was not murdered by a mobster or a gay school teacher. Still, the Eau Claire Police Department spent numerous hours documenting and pursing these so-called leads and conducted a thorough and thoughtful investigation.

On the other hand, armchair detectives would argue two young men drowning in the same lake after drinking in the same area is, on its face, evidence of foul play. In their inebriated states, however, Burrows and Noll assumed the role of auto-assassins and exponentially elevated their own risk factors. In the United States, drowning is the "fourth leading cause of accidental death, with between four thousand to five thousand incidents occurring annually." Moreover, drownings in Half Moon Lake, while infrequent, are not unusual. Since 1887, when the "young son of Widow Bell, of the Sixth ward," drowned to death, bodies of men have occasionally been recovered from the lake.[153]

CHAPTER FIVE

PERSISTENT TRENDS

Five weeks after Michael Noll disappeared, Notre Dame Freshman Chad Sharon vanished after leaving a South Bend, Indiana, off-campus party. A Wisconsin high school "all-state scholar," the Pelican Lake native was a recipient of a full academic scholarship to the prestigious university.[154]

Prior to leaving the party, Sharon declined a ride from a friend and insisted on making the six-block trek back to his campus dorm on foot. At around 4 a.m., on December 12, a young man matching Sharon's description approached a security guard at Madison Center Hospital and asked for directions to a nearby 7-Eleven store on the corner of Niles and La Salle Avenues. The convenience store was three-quarters of a mile south of the party and in the opposite direction of the Notre Dame campus.[155]

Detectives reviewed the security camera footage, but did not observe Sharon enter the 7-Eleven. Within the span of a few days, a helicopter from the Indiana State Police searched the riverbanks of the St. Joseph's River, while the Indiana Search and Rescue Team conducted a canine-assisted search. Two weeks later, investigators combed the area to the Michigan state line. The missing student was nowhere to be found.[156]

As the search for Sharon turned cold, twenty-one-year-old Nathan Herr went missing after attending a ten dollar, all drinks included evening at a Sheboygan, Wisconsin, sports pub on January 10, 2003. At about 1:30 a.m., he said goodbye to a friend as they passed Fountain Park near N. 8th Street and Erie Avenue. Herr's friend last saw him walking towards his residence, located about two miles north of the park.[157]

Unlike many of the other young men who went missing, Herr was not a college student, but a seasonal landscaper. However, the downtown area of Sheboygan where he was last seen is frequented by students. After his disappearance, the Sheboygan Police Department received tips that, on a handful of occasions, strangers had volunteered to provide rides to individuals who had been drinking near the same stretch of bars. "Those people who had rides offered to them are fine," said Deputy Sheboygan

Police Chief Robert Wojs, who added that individuals who accepted them were not harmed.[158]

On February 12, South Bend police were summoned to the banks of the St. Joseph's River under the Angela Boulevard Bridge to recover Chad Sharon's partially submerged body. The location was over a mile-and-a-half northwest of Madison Center Hospital. Had Sharon traveled north towards the Notre Dame Campus on foot, the intoxicated student may have mistakenly turned left and walked in the opposite direction of the university. Since the river's current flows south, the student probably entered the water north of Angela Boulevard, adjacent to the Holy Cross campus.[159]

An autopsy showed no indications of trauma to Sharon's body. A deputy coroner reported the seasonably cold temperatures had essentially preserved the body and the deceased's organs. The cause of death was listed as drowning. Toxicology results showed Sharon's BAC was 0.224 [160]

Prior to a memorial Mass at the Sacred Heart Basilica, police and campus officials encouraged the use of the buddy system. "If people are going off campus," said graduate student Penny Wolf, "they are telling them to go in groups and to watch out [for each other]."[161]

On February 28, with the drownings of college-age men increasingly in the news, Minneapolis police were dispatched to a report of a body snagged on debris on the east side of the Mississippi River, near an Xcel Energy hydroelectric laboratory. The corpse, first observed from the 3rd Avenue Bridge, was later identified as missing University of Minnesota business student Chris Jenkins. The body was floating face up. Typically, drowning victims are found in the prone position, unless a corpse is tangled on an obstruction and/or tossed by a strong current. On occasion, the location of the head, arms, and hand positions are sometimes "less pronounced or not present at all in victims who drowned while intoxicated" because a struggle does not occur as they disappear beneath the water.[162]

The Lone Tree Bar & Grill is just over a mile north of the Hennepin Avenue Bridge, where Jenkins' body was recovered. Investigators theorized the inebriated student went off the bridge on his own, his body becoming tangled by an obstruction. Jenkins' body was clad in the same

American-Indian Halloween costume he had donned the night he disappeared. After conducting an autopsy, the Hennepin County medical examiner determined Jenkins died from drowning, but listed the cause of death as "unknown." The medical examiner found no "discernible internal or external hemorrhaging" on the body and Jenkins' arms and legs were free of bruises or other injuries. Though legally intoxicated, the dead student's BAC was 0.12 — not excessively high. Jenkins also had 57 (mcg/ML) of gamma-hydroxybutyrate (GHB) in his system — an unusually high level that would "have rendered him in a light sleep." Although GHB is sometimes used as a "date rape drug," the substance is naturally produced by the human body. The level of GHB found in Jenkins' liver, however, suggests he either self-medicated or was drugged.[163]

The investigative timeline revealed that on the night Jenkins disappeared, a Halloween celebration began at about 8 p.m., when a keg of beer appeared at the student's residence. Three hours later, Jenkins was driven to Minneapolis' Warehouse District with other friends. Around midnight, he appeared happily buzzed and was observed dancing by himself at the Lone Tree Bar and Grill. An off-duty Minneapolis police officer, who served as the pub's bouncer, observed a wet spot on Jenkins' groin area and asked the student if he was okay. Jenkins said he had accidentally spilled the drink while dancing. A short time later, a bouncer escorted a man in American Indian garb out of the door. Since his costume had no pockets, Jenkins left without his wallet, cellular telephone, and keys. Without a jacket, which was inside the bar, he ventured into the chilly twenty-degree night.[164]

Those who believe Jenkins was a victim of foul play note he was not highly intoxicated. Being Halloween, there were likely several other patrons at the Lone Tree Bar and Grill who were, at a minimum, mildly inebriated. Yet it was Jenkins' conduct, dancing by himself with a wet spot near his groin area, which was flagged by a trained off-duty police officer/bouncer as somewhat bizarre.

"Given GHB's short shelf life," wrote retired New York City Detective Kevin Gannon, "the presence of GHB in Chris' system suggested that he died shortly after being drugged, perhaps within one to two hours."[165]

Since Jenkins was asked to leave the bar around 12:30 a.m., he could, based on Gannon's calculations, have ingested GHB prior to leaving his residence at 11 p.m. Although GHB is sometimes used to drug others without their consent, the substance is often taken voluntarily by "party and nightclub attendees and bodybuilders." GHB is consumed by individuals seeking "euphoria, increased sex drive, and tranquility." The bizarre conduct attributed to the drug's use does not necessarily point to foul play. Absent a witness stepping forward, we will likely never know whether Jenkins voluntarily or involuntarily ingested GHB.[166]

Just over a month after Jenkins' autopsy, Sheboygan police received a similar call. On March 15, a couple on a morning walk along the Lake Michigan shoreline saw a body washed ashore on the city's south side. When police arrived, they identified the deceased as Herr. The location of the recovery was about two miles south of Fountain Park. It is possible that instead of heading home, Herr decided to make another stop farther south on 8th Street prior to bar closing time at 2:30 a.m. A possible water entry location is the Sheboygan River, where the current could carry a body east into Lake Michigan.[167]

Although Herr's father believed a group was driving around the shores of Lake Michigan disposing of young men, an autopsy of Herr revealed no signs of trauma to the body. The cause of death was listed as drowning.[168]

The deaths of college-age men from other parts of the state, as well as that of a student with Wisconsin ties, spotlighted the Badger State's hard-drinking culture. In 2009, the U.S. experienced 3,517 unintentional drowning fatalities. During the same period, drowning deaths accounted for just two-tenths of one percent of U.S. homicides. An additional two hundred and seventy-one people committed suicide by drowning.[169]

Drowning is not a pleasant way to die, which may explain why so few people chose to take their own lives in this manner. After entering the water, an individual, unless intoxicated, will fight for their life and attempt to hold their breath until they need to inhale. As water enters the throat, the brain seeks to protect the lungs by inducing the larynx to spasm, which temporarily closes the trachea. Initially, very little water enters the lungs; however, the oxygen level in the brain decreases dramatically. Within half-a-minute, the lack of oxygen in the lungs causes the brain to fail.[170]

As a drowning victim losses consciousness, the individual becomes motionless in the water. As the respiratory system slowly fails, the individual descends to the bottom. Due to a lack of oxygen, a person immersed in water will convulse, their lips and skin turn blue, and frothing will typically appear in the nose and mouth. When breathing ceases, so does blood circulation, which results in cardiac arrest. If not rescued, the immersed individual dies. Depending on the temperature of the water, this agonizing process can last several minutes.[171]

According to La Crosse police, thirty-seven-year-old Gordon Stumlin committed suicide by drowning. On December 5, 2003, at about 6 p.m., Belva White, a woman who had helped raise the man, received a telephone call from a La Crosse laundromat. Sumblin, who suffered from schizophrenia, as well as alcohol and/or drug addiction issues, told White he needed help. Initially, family members believed it was possible Stumlin, who had a large amount of cash on his person, had traveled to Las Vegas.[172]

Three days later, family members reported the troubled man missing. Investigators were told Stumlin, a resident of a local group home, may have experienced a mental health crisis brought about by a friend who had committed suicide by jumping from a cliff a year to the day he went missing. Officers searched the places frequented by the missing man and attempted to trace his last steps, but found nothing.[173]

As the waterways in La Crosse became covered with ice, investigators realized it could be months before a drowning victim might surface. As spring arrived, yet another man went missing. On April 10, 2004, just after 2:30 a.m., twenty-one-year-old University of Wisconsin-La Crosse wrestler Jared Dion was last seen walking south toward a safe bus, a free transportation service that conveyed students from the downtown area back to campus, after leaving John's Bar at 109 N. 3rd Street, highly intoxicated.[174]

Twenty hours later, after the student failed to make it home, Dion's mother, Kim, appeared at the La Crosse Police Department and filed a missing person's report. Jared's girlfriend, Courtney Sherer, reported she had traveled to her parents' home in Waukesha County for the Easter weekend. Although Dion typically telephoned Sherer five times a day, the last call she received from him was on April 9. Officers and detectives began to retrace Jared's steps. An acquaintance of the missing student, John Kahl, said that on April 9 at around 10 p.m., he had visited Dion's residence, at 1141 Pine Street, with about seven or eight students. After having a few drinks, some members of the party, including Dion, took a bus from campus to John's Bar. While at the tavern, Dion conversed with Rodney Patnoe, the drummer from the Blue Olives, a band playing at John's bar. Patnoe noticed Dion was very intoxicated.[175]

Three days later, after a local newscast regarding Dion's disappearance aired, Kristine Schultz contacted La Crosse police to report she had observed a white Boston Red Sox cap, similar to the one Dion was wearing the night he vanished, on a post near the south end of a pier at Riverside Park, approximately five blocks from John's Bar. Schultz took officers to the area, but the ball cap was gone.[176]

A few hours later, Caleb Walters appeared at La Crosse PD headquarters and told an investigator he had observed a white Boston Red Sox cap on a pier post at Riverside Park. Walters thought the fitted cap looked nice and took the item home. After seeing a news report, he believed the ball cap may be related to Dion's disappearance.[177]

A short time later, La Crosse resident John Sauls contacted the police department about an earlier incident involving Dion. On September 21, 2003, at about 6:30 a.m., a newspaper delivery person knocked on Sauls' door at 2226 Barlow Street and told the homeowner a young man was sleeping on his lawn. When Officer James Kirby arrived, he made contact with Dion, who was still passed out on the wet grass. Dion was "somewhat groggy but cooperative." After a night of hard drinking, however, the student could not recall where he had been the night before or why he was sleeping on the lawn. Dion also had no shoes on and was beginning to shiver in the cold morning air. Although the officer took no enforcement action and drove him home, Dion had been blind drunk.[178]

Based on the location of Dion's ball cap, the La Crosse Fire Department and the Central Wisconsin Search and Rescue Canine Unit began dragging the Mississippi River adjacent to Riverside Park on April 14. The search was suspended at 9 p.m., and resumed the following morning. At about 7:50 a.m., the team located a body in the river just south of the Riverside Park levee. Once ashore, a La Crosse PD lieutenant recovered a wallet from the rear pants pocket of the corpse, which contained Jared Dion's Wisconsin driver's license.[179]

Dion's corpse was conveyed to Hastings, Minnesota, where Dr. Lindsay Thomas performed an autopsy. No external injuries or ligature marks were observed on the body. The clothing Dion had worn was also free of "tears, holes, abrasions." A toxicology screen ascertained the missing student's BAC was 0.27, almost three-and-a-half times the legal limit to drive. Thomas listed the cause of death as "cold water drowning."[180]

On April 16, Brian Pulver, who heard Dion's body had been recovered near Riverside Park, told investigators that, on the morning of April 10 at about 3:30 a.m., he noticed "a lone male walking westbound toward Riverside Park south of the Civic Center." This location is just four blocks from John's Bar. If Pulver's memory was correct, about an hour had passed since Dion left the tavern. While speaking to Patnoe, the drummer for the Blue Olives, Dion mentioned attending an after bar party at "an unknown location." Investigators were unable to determine if Dion attended a party or simply wandered about after bar time.[181]

The Serial Killer Conundrum

Dion's death — the seventh drowning of college-aged men in La Crosse since 1997 — began to generate a certain chatter that a serial killer was lying in wait to push intoxicated men into the Mississippi River. "The story [of a serial killer] has spread so rapidly," a well-reasoned *Green Bay Press-Gazette* Op-Ed noted, "that 1,500 people showed up to a recent community meeting to demand that local police do something to prevent more deaths."[182]

The Op-Ed cited a Harvard School of Public Health study which found that forty-four percent of college students binge drink; that alcohol consumption by college students is a contributing factor in 1,400 annual deaths; and that 500,000 Americans, ages eighteen to twenty-four, suffer injuries attributed to drinking. "Bottom line: The serial killer is not some deranged person lying in wait to shove young men into the Mississippi River. The serial killer is binge drinking, downing large quantities of alcohol in a short period of time."[183]

Just three weeks after the newspaper's thoughtful editorial had tapped down the serial killer theory, the body of Erika Dahlquist was found on a farm in Brainerd, Minnesota. The property was owned by the grandparents of William Gene Myears, who was previously charged with the second-degree murder of Dahlquist. Due to a lack of evidence, such as the missing woman's body, authorities later dropped the charges. Myears had since left the Brainerd area to work for a traveling carnival.

After being apprehended for a second time, he confessed to murdering Dahlquist during a night of heavy drinking.[184]

Although Myears was traveling with the carnival and was not in La Crosse when Dion and the others drowned, the serial killer theory was illogically rekindled. If the suspect was not Myears, the perpetrator had to be someone else. Soon, the myth spread that the police were writing off the murders as accidental deaths because inept investigators were unable to nab the wily killer — a person(s) so sophisticated that he or she could commit multiple homicides and leave behind very little if any physical evidence.[185]

On May 16, an *Associated Press* report titled "Student Deaths Haunting College Town" appeared in several newspapers. Seeking to debunk the serial killer theory, La Crosse Police Chief Edward Kondracki told the press that six of the individuals who had drowned were so intoxicated — the lowest BAC being 0.20 — that they "stumbled into the river." This opinion was not rendered by some small town cop who had ascended to the rank of police chief because of his political connections. Kondracki was a former member of the Milwaukee Police Department's command staff. In the early 1990s, Milwaukee, with a population of just under 600,000, routinely experienced more than one hundred-and-twenty annual homicides, including those attributed to serial killer Jeffrey Dahmer.[186]

La Crosse's mayor, on the other hand, viewed the deaths from the lens of a politician. "This thing is a roaring fire right now," said John Medinger. "There has to be a little voice in the back of your head some place that says, well, maybe something is going on." Based on the physical evidence, though, that "little voice" had less to do with the underlying factors behind the deaths and more to do with a politician gaging public opinion.[187]

Jared Dion's girlfriend, Courtney Sherer, also stoked the "roaring fire" by stating her boyfriend would never "strike off on his own downtown." However, John Sauls, the homeowner who discovered an intoxicated Dion passed out on his front lawn five months earlier, would take issue with Sherer's pronouncement.[188]

The unsupportable hunches of the armchair sleuths depicted the killer as a police impersonator or "a disgruntled hospital worker knocking people out with chloroform." Another theory held that a shapely young woman lured the intoxicated men to the river before shoving them in.[189]

Yet, if the killer had kidnapped the men, the victims would have likely struggled, sustained at least significant bruising, and/or their bodies would have displayed ligature markings at the autopsies. As it relates to the fatal attraction theory of the shapely woman, witnesses had observed Anthony Skifton and Dion walking alone towards a body of water.

Nonetheless, news about the drowning deaths continued to trickle in. On June 7, Scott Glinski, an executive at the technology company Skyward, maneuvered his thirty-five foot Carver yacht from La Crosse's Mississippi River based Pettibone Boat Club, where he had stopped to refuel. As he traveled north, a bass boat came by Glinski's location "at a high rate of speed" two hundred yards south of the Cass Street Bridge. In the bass boat's wake, Glinski saw something "pop" to the surface. When he moved the boat closer to get a better look, Glinski believed the object was a "human body."[190]

After calling the police, a large barge headed directly for the floating corpse. Glinski raised the barge's operator by radio and requested the vessel divert course. Within a matter of minutes, a boat with a police officer arrived.[191]

Having commandeered a ride from the staff at the La Crosse Municipal Boat Harbor, the officer took notice of the white male's badly decomposed remains. A boat from the La Crosse Fire Department transported the corpse to shore just west of the fire department's training tower. An assistant medical examiner then removed a wallet from the right front pants pocket of the deceased and found Gordon Stumlin's identification. The wallet further contained a "large amount of money" that the troubled man reportedly possessed on the date he went missing.[192]

Two days later, the pathologist performing the autopsy found no trauma or other injuries to Stumlin's body. Based on the totality of the circumstances — the distress call to White and the death of his friend a year earlier — the cause of death was listed as drowning and believed to be a suicide.[193]

Here, the suicide determination was the probable reason for Stumlin's demise. If he had been a victim of foul play, the large amount of cash in his wallet would have certainly been taken. Moreover, Stumlin did not meet the criteria of the typical drowning victim: He apparently wasn't intoxicated, was nearing middle-age, and was at a laundromat, not a nightclub or tavern.

The media spotlight concerning the strange deaths of college-age men took a short respite as the warm summer air arrived. The conspiracy theorists failed to note that, if a serial killer did exist, he or she routinely took long summer vacations. Surprisingly, the adherents to the serial killer theory had yet to suspect a college faculty member who spent summers out of town, or construction workers idled during the winter months.

CHAPTER SIX
A KILLER WITH RANK

The summer of 2004 passed without fanfare. After Labor Day, however, another college student drowned. The incident occurred about six blocks north of the UW – Eau Claire campus. In this instance, a witness saw a man acting rather oddly while standing near a body of water.

On September 12, at 3:26 a.m., twenty-two-year-old Chris Lokken observed UW-Eau Claire student Jesse Miller standing on the Chippewa River shoreline beneath the Lake Street Bridge. Finding Miller's conduct somewhat unusual, Lokken flagged down a passing squad car. From a distance, a police officer shouted questions to the student, who had already entered the river. Miller then shouted back, "You have no idea what's going on," and moved further into the river until Lokken and the officer lost sight of him.[194]

The Chippewa River is not as wide and its currents are not as treacherous as the mighty Mississippi. Depending on the amount of rainfall, entering the Chippewa River without a floatation device is not necessarily a death sentence, especially in early September when the water temperature is relatively warm. In the summer months, college students routinely tube the river from Phoenix Park to the UW–Eau Claire campus.

At sunrise, searchers found Miller's body in the river just south of the Lake Street Bridge. Retracing the deceased student's steps, investigators learned he had visited at least two taverns on Water Street, a location with a stretch of taverns nine blocks southwest of the bridge. Just before midnight, fellow student Paul Diedrich spoke to Miller at Shenanigans, a tavern at 415 Water Street. "He seemed so normal," said Diedrich. "He was out having a good time. We found no difference in him."[195]

About an hour later, UW-Eau Claire senior Jon Gaulke observed Miller at the Pioneer Tavern, a half-block east of Shenanigans. Gaulke, however, did not speak with Miller. Unfortunately, one of Miller's described personality traits may have cost him his life. The deceased student's sister, Becca, told the UW-Eau Claire *Spectator* one of her brother's strengths "was that he never followed a crowd or cared what anyone thought of him."[196]

Toxicology samples taken during the autopsy put Miller's BAC at 0.22, which, according to Eau Claire Police Department Community Relations Officer Jack Corey, "is a significant blood alcohol level." An individual this intoxicated, Corey reasoned, " would typically need to have someone with him."[197]

On September 12, bar time in Eau Claire was at 2:30 a.m. Yet almost an hour passed before Chris Lokken observed Miller under the Lake Street Bridge. This gap in the investigative timeline suggests the student may have visited a house party on his way home from Water Street.

A *Spectator* report also mentioned a previous death related to an area bridge. Almost a year earlier, Jacob Libby, a twenty-year-old student from Minnesota, died "after sustaining injuries from a fall off the Water Street Bridge," adjacent to the UW–Eau Claire campus. Police said Libby had consumed alcohol.[198]

Although very tragic, Jesse Miller's death proved that intoxicated students, for whatever reasons, seemingly entered bodies of water on their own volition. Clearly, Miller was not lured to the banks of the Chippewa River by a shapely female or abducted by a police impersonator. Instead, Chris Lokken's astute observation of the area beneath the Lake Street Bridge had ripped a hole through the serial killer theory.

Well documented in the UW — Eau Claire campus newspaper, the student's demise resulted in a year-long hiatus of alcohol-fueled drowning deaths. Residing in Hastings, Minnesota, at the time of Miller's death, former Eau Claire resident Josh Snell either did not hear the news, or disregarded the dangers of binge drinking.

On June 11, 2005, twenty-two-year-old Snell arrived in Eau Claire to attend a wedding held at a hotel near W. Clairemont Avenue and Stein Boulevard, just to the south of UW-Eau Claire's upper campus. At around 10 p.m., Snell telephoned his former girlfriend, Abigail Hafner, who arrived at the hotel and drove Snell from the reception to Mogie's Pub on Water Street. Snell soon joined a pool game with three other men. At around 11 p.m., Hafner told Snell she was making the block-long trek to the Pioneer bar. Snell indicated he would meet Hafner at the Pioneer at the conclusion of the pool shoot, but he never made the trip.[199]

The following afternoon, two of Snell's friends, Matthew Starland and Chad Roth, contacted the Eau Claire Police Department and reported him missing. Prior to leaving the wedding reception, Snell did not notify his friends he was leaving for Water Street. Starland was concerned because Snell was known to walk off on his own during bouts of binge drinking. Starland then telephoned Snell, who said he had walked to Water Street. However, instead of traveling to Water Street, Starland, Roth, Justin Mack and Karen Barthels stopped by the Happy Hallow bar in Altoona.[200]

At 10:49 p.m., Snell sent Starland a text message and asked him to visit Water Street before he went "$200 in the hole" from losing at pool. Barthels left the Happy Hollow first and called Starland to report Snell was at Brother's Pub in the 300 block of Water Street, shooting pool with three unknown men. After arriving at Brother's, the friends grabbed a table. At around midnight, Snell said he was going to get some popcorn, but never returned. The following morning, Snell failed to give his sister, Joanna, a ride to Minnesota. Hearing that his son was a no-show, Snell's father, Robert, telephoned Starland, who indicated Josh had walked away from his friends at Brother's Pub.[201]

Investigators contacted Abigail Hafner, who said Snell had called her cell phone between 2:00–2:30 a.m. During the conversation, Snell sounded "scared" and said he really "screwed up" and was in trouble with the police. The intoxicated-sounding caller told Hafner he was in "Eau Claire Park," east of her Water Street apartment, and was crawling in the bushes.[202]

Prior to calling Hafner, police learned that Snell had also telephoned Cody Kopp at 1:38 a.m., 1:39 a.m. and 1:41 a.m. During the last call, Snell "sounded drunk" and left a message that consisted of him singing a song in German. Kopp further related Snell frequently called when he was drunk, which was why Kopp was unconcerned about the voice mail.[203]

Based, in part, on Snell's inebriated gibberish, it is possible to interpret why he was upset and in trouble with the "police." Kopp's roommate, Ben Rust, was a colleague of Snell's at Russ Davis Wholesale in Inver Grove, Minnesota. It is possible Snell, knowing that he was highly intoxicated at almost 2 a.m., realized he would not make it to work at 10:30 a.m. In an effort to have Rust cover for him, it is reasonable to conclude Snell telephoned Kopp to alert his roommate. In fact, when Snell failed to show up for work, Rust was "subbing" for him. In his intoxicated state,

Snell may have told Hafner he was having trouble getting in touch with "Kopp"; whereby, the word was misinterpreted as a reference to "cops."[204]

Another friend of the missing man, Jeffrey Leinberger, told police Snell had a history of simply walking off when he binge drank. During a visit to Eau Claire two weeks before he went missing, Snell, Leinberger, and a group of friends were at the Happy Hallow tavern in Altoona. Less than an hour later, Snell disappeared without notice. While out with his friends, Leinberger received a call from Kristine Dryer, who said Snell had left the Happy Hallow, walked four miles to his truck, and drove to her home in Eau Claire. Leinberger told detectives Snell's disappearing act worried him because his friend was "irresponsible when he has been drinking."[205]

Nonetheless, investigators from the Eau Claire Police Department pulled out all the stops. Snell's cellular telephone provider, T-Mobile, was contacted. Telephone records confirmed the incoming and outgoing calls to Kopp and Hafner. Officials at T-Mobile attempted to triangulate the final call, but were unable to ascertain Snell's last known location. Associated Bank provided investigators access to Snell's ATM records, but no withdrawals had occurred since his disappearance.[206]

Based on Snell's statement to Hafner that he was in "Eau Claire Park" east of her Water Street apartment, investigators surmised the missing man may have meant Owen Park, which runs along the west bank of the Chippewa River from Water to Lake Streets. On June 13, officers searching the park located a plaid shirt near the tennis courts, directly across the street from the UW-Eau Claire campus. A digital photo of the shirt was shown to Hafner, who said it matched the garment worn by Snell when she last saw him.[207]

The Eau Claire Police Department requested the assistance of Dunn County Sheriff's Deputy Dale Dohms and his trained bloodhound, Jet. Upon arriving at Owen Park, Dohms was offered a duffel bag that belonged to Snell. Starting from the point where the shirt was discovered, about a football field west of the river, Jet tracked eastbound toward the riverbank and ran into the water. Jet was so certain of the scent track that he would not leave the water. Dohms reported Jet's actions meant someone with Snell's scent had entered the Chippewa River.[208]

An hour later, a friend of Snell's, Eric Long, was walking the river bank and observed a black, long-sleeved t-shirt next to the bike trail at the base of the Lake Street Bridge, five blocks north of the Owen Park tennis courts. Investigators soon discovered the t-shirt was originally found by a firefighter and tossed towards the bike path. The bloodhound was taken to this location and traced Snell's scent from the Lake Street Bridge to the location near Water Street.[209]

The black t-shirt, which sported the logo of the musical group Target Market, was purchased by Snell at a Twin Cities concert. The fire department was summoned to the area of Owen Park and began dragging the river.[210]

As some of Snell's friend watched the fire crews work the river, Krysta Maurice told police she was with the missing man at Brother's Pub. Also at the park was Chad Roth, who told an officer the t-shirt was probably Snell's. Kristine Dryer, a former girlfriend of Snell's, told an investigator the missing man previously said that, due to his drinking problem, he was "not good enough" for her. Another friend, Tiffany Kettinger, said Snell "drank a lot," was "very moody," and his mood swings "displeased most of her friends."[211]

Nevertheless, the June 13 drag operation of the Chippewa River near Owen Park did not result in a recovery. The search for Snell continued. Two days later, members of the Pure Water Paddles Kayaking Club observed a body floating in the river about fifty feet south of the Short Street Bridge, two-and-a-half miles downstream from Owen Park. The shirtless corpse was face down in the water and snagged on a fallen tree on the west bank of the river. Due to the strong current, a police sergeant sawed through the branches of the tree. A pole-hook was attached to the belt of the deceased and the body was pulled from the water.[212]

Once on shore, a wallet was removed from the rear pants pocket of the corpse, which held the Minnesota driver's license of Joshua Snell. The body was transported from Hobbs Landing to Sacred Heart Hospital. John Snell soon came to the hospital's morgue and identified the deceased as his brother, Josh.[213]

The following day an autopsy was performed by Dr. Hofer, who observed no signs of trauma to Snell's body. The upper torso and face, which had been snagged to the tree and exposed to air, was black due to decomposition and lividity. A large amount of fresh water found in the lungs was consistent with fresh water drowning. A toxicology test, conducted the by Wisconsin State Laboratory of Hygiene, listed Snell's BAC at 0.20.[214]

Sadly, Josh Snell's friends — the persons closest to him — never intervened or cajoled him to seek treatment for what appeared to be a significant drinking problem. What became clear, however, was a killer was indeed at work in Eau Claire. He was a high-ranking figure who may have had a hand in the deaths of Jesse Miller and Snell. His name was Captain Morgan.

CHAPTER SEVEN
TROUBLED YOUNG MEN

Over the course of the past decade, several myths concerning the strange deaths of young men in Wisconsin have been perpetuated by those in the media and by individuals who have failed to examine each case in its totality. One such media personality is Eugene Kane, the former columnist at the *Milwaukee Journal Sentinel.*

Kane, a person who views virtually every issue through the lens of race, fired off a column in 2013 "about drunken white males who stumble into a river" and then wondered, in print, "why black males who drink a lot don't end up in the river and why his particular racial angle seldom gets discussed."[215]

As usual, Kane's racial bluster about these drownings was dead wrong. Not all of the victims are "drunken young white males" who "go out on a bender." Moreover, had Kane done some basic research, he would have discovered a handful of newspaper articles that addressed the issue of alcohol abuse being the underlying factor in the strange deaths of these young men. Nine years prior to Kane's ridiculous column, the uncle of drowning victim Anthony Skifton, La Crosse Police Lieutenant Dan Marcou, told the press his community was "like an alcoholic" who would rather believe a serial killer is on the loose "than admit it's got a drinking problem."[216]

Another myth is that all of the drowning cases, as well as other unexplained deaths, have occurred in college towns. "Why is it," a woman recently asked me, "that these drownings only take place in La Crosse?" The answer is easy: They don't. These strange deaths have taken place throughout the Badger State and not all involve drowning deaths. Some are probable suicides and a very small number may involve foul play. While substance abuse is often linked to suicide deaths, other issues, such as depression, bipolar disorder, schizophrenia, and post-traumatic stress, are also contributing factors.[217]

Depression played an underlying role in the demise of Japanese citizen Kenji Ohmi, who had attended an English as a second language school in Madison. The twenty-year-old did not drink alcohol and did not use drugs. Far from home and unable to communicate with most of his fellow students, he developed an acute case of homesickness.[218]

One of Ohmi's roommates at the Wisconsin Second Language Institute, Seokwon Hwang, last saw the Japanese student at 5 a.m. on Saturday, January 28, 2006. Ohmi was in the kitchen of their small dormitory apartment on N. Hamilton Street.[219]

Hwang told an officer Ohmi was "a loner" and was "nervous and shy and insecure." Although his roommate had taken his passport, Hwang found it odd Ohmi had left both of his wallets behind.[220]

When the Japanese student failed to appear on Sunday, a resident manager of the Hamilton Street dormitory, Jessica Harmaty, contacted the owner of the school, who instructed her to wait until the following morning to contact the police.[221]

When Ohmi had failed to show up for class, Harmaty searched his room in an effort to ascertain his whereabouts. One of the items she located was a journal. A student at the school translated the journal's contents and discovered two disturbing entries. On January 8, Ohmi wrote he wanted to kill himself, but "didn't have the strength to follow through." In another entry, the missing student said his peers frowned upon him because he could not communicate well.[222]

Harmaty further told investigators Ohmi was an introvert who had very few interactions with students or instructors. Officers from the Madison Police Department checked with area hospitals, the Dane County Jail, and the local detox center, but none had any contact with the missing student.[223]

The following day, detectives interviewed Eduardo Alvarez Perez, a foreign student from Panama, who also resided with Ohmi. On January 27 at 9 p.m., Perez planned to attend a party two doors down the hall. Just before leaving, Ohmi had turned in for the evening. When Perez returned to the apartment at 6 a.m., the Japanese student was sleeping on a sofa in the living room. When Ohmi awoke, Perez greeted him before going to sleep. When Perez emerged from his room at about 11:30 a.m., his roommate was gone. A check of the building's surveillance system showed Ohmi left his apartment at 6:31 a.m. He was wearing a black outer garment, jeans, and white tennis shoes. When Ohmi failed to return by late Sunday afternoon, Perez contacted the resident manager,

Harmaty.[224]

Several Madison Police Department officers conducted an extensive search for Ohmi. The police also released information bulletins to the media and kept the Japanese consulate in Chicago appraised of the situation. Yet it seemed as if Ohmi had fallen off the face of the earth.[225]

In the short term, some reports of possible sightings of the missing student trickled in. On the evening of January 30, a Madison Fire Department lieutenant said he had observed an Asian male matching Ohmi's description at the fire station on Midvale Boulevard and Regent Street. However, investigators determined the Asian male was nine inches taller than the missing student.[226]

In early February, a driver for the bus company Van Galder, Richard Rebout, said a passenger matching Ohmi's description boarded his bus near the University of Wisconsin Memorial Union. The man sought to travel to Chicago and had trouble communicating with Rebout. A white female, fluent in Japanese, explained the fare was $24. The man matching Ohmi's description later transferred buses in Janesville. Rebout said the Asian man was five-foot-three, wearing a black coat that extended to the thigh area.[227]

In the interim, the Japanese consulate spoke to Ohmi's mother. Initially, she told a consulate representative her son "had no problems." A short time later, Ohmi's mother telephoned the consulate to report that she had gone through her son's journals and found entries stating her son had contemplated suicide prior to leaving for the U.S. Ohmi's mother further said her son had battled serious bouts of depression since age twelve.[228]

Unaware of the number of Asian males attending the University of Wisconsin, as well as the missing Japanese student's height, other reports of Ohmi again materialized. A couple reported seeing a man matching his description at a January 29 Mozart concert conducted at the UW Humanities building. A reporter for the *Capital Times* newspaper believed he had spotted Ohmi at Strictly Discs, a store that carries compact discs for aging baby boomers. In both instances, however, the Asian men were described as being five-foot-eight.[229]

Anonymous sources told investigators they observed Ohmi at the Grace Shelter, just a block from the Wisconsin State Capitol Building, and at a food give away at the First United Methodist Church on Wisconsin Avenue. Detectives visited each location and determined the sightings were false.[230]

Although he had absolutely no connections to the city, two people reported seeing the Japanese student in Milwaukee. On March 2, the Madison police received another anonymous tip that Ohmi was observed standing in front of the University of Wisconsin – Milwaukee engineering building. UW-Milwaukee police posted fliers around campus, but nothing ever came of the tip.[231]

Four weeks later, a former employee of Milwaukee's St. Vincent-DePaul Society called to report that a contact, a homeless man named "Bob," caught a glimpse of Ohmi in the company of an Asian female near the Marquette University campus. As Bob posted fliers of the missing student inside the Milwaukee Central Library, an Asian woman approached him and said she was Ohmi's mother. About an hour later, Bob observed the same woman with the missing student seven blocks west of the library. The tipster further told investigators he believed Bob was "mentally unstable."[232]

The last alleged sighting of Ohmi came on April 25, when an officer was dispatched to a report that a man matching the missing student's description was staying at an apartment near downtown Madison. An officer and a detective made contact with the apartment's occupant, but nothing unusual was found. For the next eight weeks, the investigation into the missing student turned cold.[233]

Then, on June 19, windsurfer Michael Cockrem spotted an object floating about two hundred yards from shore in the 1200 block of Sherman Avenue in Madison. As he moved closer, Cockrem could see a human body. The windsurfer immediately went to shore and contacted lifeguards at the Tenney Park beach.[234]

When officers arrived, Cockrem said he had observed a corpse floating face down in the water, ten houses south of Tenney Park beach. The responding officer was offered a ride in a citizen's boat. They located the bloated body, which was clothed in a black sweatshirt, with the hood pulled over the head, and white tennis shoes.[235]

A crew from the Madison Fire Department's Water Rescue Unit pulled the body from the water, placed it in a body bag, and conveyed the corpse to the Dane County morgue for an autopsy. Although the body was badly decomposed, the face was recognizable as that of an Asian male. The deceased was wearing white tennis shoes and denim blue jeans "shredded" by an apparent boat prop. Investigators located Ohmi's Japanese passport in a pocket of the black jacket. The cause of death was fresh water drowning. A toxicology report completed by the Wisconsin State Crime Laboratory indicated Ohmi was sober when he died.[236]

Having left his apartment without a wallet, detectives theorized the suicidal Japanese student simply walked onto Lake Mendota until the thin ice gave way. The cold water likely caused hypothermia to set in within a minute, which reduced the resistance to struggle. After he drowned, gases typically caused by decomposition were suppressed by the cold water. As a result, Ohmi's body remained at the bottom of the lake until a hard ice formed.

Ohmi's Madison journal entries and Jesse Miller's delusional rant to police on the banks of the Chippewa River enabled investigators to quickly close the books on both of these death investigations. Absent such clear and convincing evidence, detectives inspect the totality of the circumstances. When a sudden death lacks a clear and concise causal effect, such as journal entries, suicide notes, or statements, a consensus generally emerges during briefings between detectives and their supervisors. On occasion, these gatherings are similar to a graduate school thesis or dissertation defense with a lieutenant or other detectives challenging an investigator's interpretation of the facts.

During my tenure with the Milwaukee Police Department, many of these briefings were conducted in "the Dahmer room" — a former storage area that became the nerve center for the investigation into the largest number of homicides linked to a single perpetrator in city history. Unlike the highly unbelievable police procedural television programs, where analysts have access to health and financial databases, the Dahmer room was low-tech. Yet this was the place where the rubber met the road. After all, if a detective offered a theory or motive unsupported by evidence, ridicule by one's peers might follow. Having been retired now for over a decade, I often wonder how today's millennial generation investigators would have fared during a handful of the contentious briefings in the 1990s.

Though the Dahmer room briefings acted as a filter to ferret out poorly conceived theories, their principal purpose was information shar-ing. Detectives who brought little to these gatherings sometimes drew the ire of a homicide lieutenant, who might ask, "What the hell are you doing out there?" On occasion, these briefings also offered a venue to bounce ideas off each other. While detectives are encouraged to think outside the box, input from one's peers often corralled investigators who strayed too far.

In academic circles, peer review of articles and books challenges the author. In police work, input from peers comes in a variety of forms, such as station house chats, performance evaluation or briefings. When inves-tigators are no longer subjected to direct or indirect oversight from their supervisors or peers, they sometimes surmise theories that would not pass the Dahmer room smell test.

In 2006, two former New York City Police Department detectives, Kevin Gannon and Anthony Duarte, began vigorously exploring the drowning deaths of young men throughout the country through the lens of the serial killer phenomena. On April 28, the two former detectives visited the Eau Claire Police Department.

After being met in a briefing room by a lieutenant, Gannon and Du-arte identified themselves as acting NYPD detectives and said they were investigating a homicide in New York City, which had similarities to the drowning deaths in Eau Claire, La Crosse, and the Twin Cities. Duarte also displayed a badge.[237]

After the detectives met with an Eau Claire PD deputy chief, Gan-non and Duarte told the lieutenant they were assigned to "Bronx Homi-cide," but had been hired by the family of Pat McNeill, of New York, and were working "independently." After obtaining a map of Eau Claire, the two former detectives left the building. An Eau Claire police sergeant contacted the NYPD and learned both Gannon and Duarte "were re-tired officers from the NYPD and currently were civilians."[238]

A short time later, Gannon and Duarte returned to the Eau Claire Police Department. The two men asked for the contact information for Josh Snell's girlfriend and the elderly woman who received the unwanted visit from Michael Noll. Since neither was a sworn investigator, the Eau Claire Police Department refused to turn over any reports and advised the former detectives they would need to file an open records request.[239]

Gannon began speculating about the presence of a possible serial killer after the body of a twenty-year-old man was pulled from New York City's East River. Patrick McNeill, Jr. was last seen alive on February 16, 1997, after leaving The Dapper Dog bar shortly before midnight. The "highly intoxicated" McNeill told his friends he was heading for his Fordham University dorm room. Police officials told the press the business student was later observed "staggering east on 90th Street," on his way to a subway platform.[240]

Seven weeks later, McNeill's corpse was found floating face up in the East River, near a pier at Bay Ridge in Brooklyn, by a crew from the Army Corps of Engineers. An autopsy report noted McNeill suffered no broken bones, and had no signs of head trauma or other physical injuries. The manner of death was listed as "undetermined."[241]

As one of the case detectives, Gannon found inconsistencies in the autopsy report. After reviewing photographs of McNeill's body, the detective spotted what he believed was a ligature mark on the deceased student's neck and small black spots on the body. The pathologist, however, did not note any ligature marks and attributed the dark spots to decomposition. Gannon also argued that fly larvae, found in McNeill's pubic region, suggested he had been dead prior to entering the water.[242]

By 2006, Gannon had admittedly become obsessed with the McNeill investigation and joined forces with Duarte, who had retired from the NYPD. The two men also probed the suspicious death of Christopher Jenkins, as well as the drownings of other young men in Eau Claire and La Crosse. On an apparent shoestring budget, the retired detectives' alleged misrepresentations of their professional credentials to officials from the Eau Claire Police Department suggested they were cutting corners.[243]

As one might expect, the investigations conducted by the two retired NYPD detectives failed to deter the actual killer, whose cunning emanated from the interior of a bottle. The tragic death of a University of Wisconsin–La Crosse basketball player is, unfortunately, one such example.

By all accounts, Lucas "Luke" Homan was a very likable young man. His father, Jerry, was drafted in the eighth round by the New York Knicks after a standout career under the tutelage of legendary coach Al McGuire at Marquette. Like his father, Luke was a solid athlete. He quarterbacked his high school football team at Brookfield Central and excelled at basketball. After his freshman year at UW–Milwaukee, a Division I school, he transferred to UW–La Crosse's Division III program and became a member of the basketball team. Like too many college-age men, Homan occasionally consumed large quantities of alcohol in a relatively short period of time.[244]

On Friday, September 30, 2006, at around 10 a.m., Homan, along with a few friends, visited the grounds of La Crosse's annual Oktoberfest for the opening of the Golden Keg, a tradition that kicks-off the weekend-long event. The students later procured a keg of beer and began partying at an apartment in the 1500 block of Main Street.[245]

A few hours later, Homan, described by a visitor to the apartment as inebriated, went to his room to take a nap. Prior to dozing off at 4 p.m., Homan sent an e-mail to UW – Madison student Lindsey McCormick. While the overall content was "upbeat," the message contained several spelling and grammatical errors, inconsistent with e-mails sent when Homan was sober.[246]

At about 6 p.m., three friends from the Milwaukee area, Brian Hillus, Nick Waldera, and Ryan Schmidt, arrived in La Crosse and woke Homan up. Hillus told investigators he could tell Luke had "already started drinking." The student's friends had traveled to La Crosse to participate in a Saturday golf tournament.[247]

At about 7 p.m., Homan and his visiting friends made the mile drive to the Vibe, a bar located at 332 Jay Street. While at the tavern, Waldera said Luke took a break from drinking because he was becoming intoxicated. "He was drunk," said Waldera, "but knew what was going on."[248]

Somewhere between 9-10 p.m., Waldera, Hillus and Schmidt left for the Long Horns bar. Homan remained at the Vibe with a few other friends, including Austin Scott. Investigators believed Scott was the last person to have contact with Homan at the Vibe. The following day, Scott reportedly told acquaintances he had been involved in some sort of altercation at the bar and was struck in the head with a beer bottle.[249]

As detectives attempted to track down Scott, La Crosse police conducted an extensive canvass of the city's downtown entertainment district. In all, officers contacted forty-nine businesses, searched for surveillance videos, checked dumpsters and scoured the banks of the Mississippi River. Based on my thirty years of law enforcement experience, the resources dedicated to this canvass were similar to those typically expended during a high-profile homicide investigation.[250]

In an effort to interview Scott, an investigator tracked down the student's cellular telephone number. A call placed to the phone was answered, but when the investigator asked to discuss Homan's disappearance, the call was promptly terminated. After the detective left a voice message, the telephone was turned off.[251]

A half-hour later, Scott appeared at La Crosse PD headquarters. An investigator noted the student appeared "very upset and nervous" and "kept sitting with his head down and both hands over his mouth and nose area." Detectives familiar with the Reid Technique of Interviewing and Interrogation are aware individuals who place their hands over their mouths or eyes are being, at a minimum, guarded. When coupled with looking down at the floor, these two non-verbal indicators point to evasiveness.[252]

During the short interview, Scott told a detective that Homan was involved in a confrontation with three men at the Vibe. A short time later, Luke and the three men left the bar. The three men later returned, confronted Scott, and asked, "Where's your buddy?" One of the men struck Scott in the head with a beer bottle. Scott told a detective he then left the Vibe and walked home.[253]

Prior to interviewing Scott, investigators caught a break. While following up on a report the intoxicated student was involved in an altercation at the Vibe, a detective learned Scott was contacted by an officer outside the downtown Radisson Hotel.[254]

On September 29, at about 8:30 p.m., La Crosse County Sheriff's Deputy Chris Fabry, on horseback patrolling the Oktoberfest celebration, was leaving an area near Riverside Park when he observed a college-age white male, later identified as Scott, staggering across the street. Scott walked behind the Radisson Hotel and, intoxicated to the point he could no longer walk, sat down between two cars in the hotel's parking lot. The deputy observed an injury to Scott's head and summoned medical assistance. Fabry's report noted Scott was "unaware that he was injured" and continued to mumble, "I'm alright." A portable breath test pegged Scott's BAC at 0.26. Spots of blood were also found on the intoxicated student's shoes. Prior to the fire department conveying him to the Franciscan-Shemp detoxification unit, the deputy smartly seized Scott's shoes as evidence.[255]

In possession of information that showed Scott was being untruthful, investigators conducted a recorded interview. Besides omitting he had been taken to detox, investigators noted Scott had provided them with a false date of birth and address. When confronted with the earlier lies, Scott was asked to "start over" and tell the truth.[256]

Again, Scott said he was at the Vibe with Luke. Since he had been drinking, events were "kind of a blur," although Scott recalled Homan speaking with three men. Later, the three men came back into the Vibe and asked about Luke's whereabouts. One of the men then struck Scott in the head with a beer bottle.[257]

Scott further told investigators he had "no idea how he got to the Radisson" and did not recall being taken to detox. He remembered, however, leaving the detox center after being provided with a voucher for a taxi cab ride to his residence. Once inside his apartment, Scott said he immediately went to bed. After he awoke, he telephoned a friend, who indicated Luke had failed to return home.[258]

After a short break to compare notes, investigators conducted a second recorded interview. When questioned about his clothing, Scott said he was wearing the same shoes he wore on the date he was taken to detox. When a detective observed red spots on one of his shoes, Scott remarked the spot that was on a shoe lace was from juice, but indicated a red spot on the tongue of the shoe "could be blood." Although Deputy Fabry had previously seized Scott's original pair of shoes, La Crosse detectives further confiscated the shoes Scott had worn to the interview. When asked why he had provided false information to investigators, Scott replied, "I just didn't want you guys to know I was at the hospital. I don't know. I'm sorry. I apologize."[259]

Aware that Scott — the last person to see Homan — was contacted leaving Riverside Park, the area became the focal point of the search. As investigators grilled Scott, Sarg, a cadaver dog from the Wisconsin Canine Search and Rescue team, tracked Homan's scent from the Vibe bar to Riverside Park. In possession of Scott's shoes, a bloodhound also traced Scott's scent from the Vibe bar and "ended up at the same point" as Homan. A dive team dragged the river and officers on shore conducted an extensive search, but found no evidence of the missing student.[260]

On October 2, the search near Riverside Park resumed. After launching a boat from the municipal harbor, representatives from the People and Paws Rescue Team and a cadaver dog searched the levee area near Riverside Park. When the dog hit on the location, deputies from the La Crosse County Sheriff's Department conducted an underwater search of the levee. At 9:45 a.m., a member of the dive team, William Powell, located Homan's corpse in ten feet of water twenty feet from shore. Homan's body was taken to Hastings, Minnesota, for an autopsy.[261]

During the autopsy, an investigator noted the deceased was still clad in the maroon UW–La Crosse sweatshirt, blue jeans, and New Balance athletic shoes. A brown wallet, which was recovered from Homan's right front pants pocket, contained his identification, a credit card, and $40 in cash. An examination of the body showed no significant injuries or ligature marks. A toxicology test listed Homan's BAC at 0.32. The cause of death was fresh water drowning.[262]

In the interim, officers interviewed Josh Berna, who claimed to have observed Homan enter The Library bar on September 30 between 1-1:30 a.m. Berna said Homan was "very intoxicated" and was wearing a Milwaukee Brewers' ball cap and black fleece pullover. The clothing description was inconsistent with the one provided by Homan's friends. Based on the clothing discrepancies, detectives suspected Berna had misidentified the man as Homan.[263]

On October 3, Scott appeared at La Crosse PD headquarters for a third recorded interview. While his statement remained relatively similar, Scott said he was "very drunk" while at the Vibe bar and being struck in the head with a beer bottle was something that he may have dreamt. Investigators believed Scott was "still being deceptive and appeared to be withholding information."[264]

At this point, Austin Scott became the focus of the investigation. A detective contacted his roommate, Joseph Mesarchik, who spent the night off campus and had not seen Scott on the morning Homan went missing. During a telephone call later that day, however, Scott told Mesarchik he had been hit by a rock, not a beer bottle, during an altercation.[265]

On October 10, Scott agreed to meet with investigators from the La Crosse PD and the Wisconsin Department of Criminal Investigation. When confronted with the bloodhound scent trails, as well as the deputy and employees of the Radisson Hotel seeing him exit Riverside Park, Scott did not deny being in the park, but simply could not recall what occurred while he was there. Scott requested a "lie detector test" to determine if he was, in fact, inside Riverside Park. A test was scheduled for the following morning.[266]

At 10 a.m., Scott again appeared at La Crosse PD headquarters and submitted to a voice stress test administered by an investigator from the La Crosse County Sheriff's Department. The final result indicated Scott was "being deceptive during the test and was blocking out the incident that took place in the park."[267]

Armed with the results of the voice stress test, investigators immediately confronted Scott. The student "cupped his hands over his face and put his head down on the table and began to cry." He then stated he would "never leave him [Homan] in the water." When asked to elaborate, Scott did not respond. When asked why he would not articulate what he meant, Scott replied he was concerned what Homan's friends and family, as well as his own family, might think of him. When asked what upset him most, Scott answered "that Luke's gone" and, after pausing for a second, explained "and I was there and didn't do anything."[268]

Scott went on to state his "best guess is that he [Homan] tripped." Scott also said he would "never know for sure if that's what happened" because he "couldn't remember." Scott then bowed his head, began to cry, and said "something to the effect that he [Homan] fell in and he couldn't do anything about it." When asked if he had observed Homan trip and fall into the water, Scott did not respond.[269]

Highly intoxicated while inside Riverside Park, Scott said the best he could do was offer two scenarios. In one instance, he and Luke walked to the park and were sitting on a bench, but from that point forward he could not recall anything. In the second scenario, they were walking in the park, but Scott could not remember anything additional. Scott explained that several different images "went through his head," but he did not know which one was true.[270]

Hoping to jog his memory and address any mental health questions, investigators referred Scott to a counselor. Although the investigation into Homan's death was listed as "continuing," the memory of Scott, heavily clouded by a high degree of intoxication, brought the case to a screeching halt. In the near future, however, the City of La Crosse would install surveillance cameras in Riverside Park and at other key locations.

Though Kenji Ohmi and Luke Homan had succumbed to different demons, one thing was crystal clear: A serial killer was not responsible for either man's demise. In many instances, individual human beings are often their own worst enemies. When problems, such as mental health issues or alcohol abuse, are left unaddressed, premature death is sometimes the end result.

CHAPTER EIGHT
REVIEW & REVIVAL

Although Luke Homan's tragic death was unrelated to a serial killer, the public's concern pertaining to the drownings in La Crosse rose to a crescendo. Three days after Homan's body was pulled from the Mississippi River, a columnist at the *Advance-Titian*, the student newspaper of the University of Wisconsin – Oshkosh, reasoned the deaths in La Crosse were "a tragedy" that "no coincidence could explain."[271]

Oshkosh has "an active college bar scene in a hard-drinking Wisconsin city with a large river nearby," wrote Dan Shafer. "But we never hear about a student involved in an alcohol-induced drowning in the Fox [River]."[272]

Ignoring the evidence, and perpetuating the myth that all of the drowning deaths occurred in just one Wisconsin college town, Shafer, a student at a university 150 miles east of La Crosse with no investigative experience, weighed in. "Could this just be coincidence? Could alcohol have impaired their [the deceased students] judgment so much that the most logical thing to do would be to go wandering alone near the Mississippi? I believe that this is something more that [sic] mere coincidental occurrences."[273]

With the Homan investigation ongoing, and unaware of Scott's presence in Riverside Park, Shafter cited the remarks of Dan Borchard, who said his college roommate "was not the type of guy to go off on his own." In essence, had Scott, as investigators suspected, traveled with Homan to Riverside Park, Borchard's comments, while correct, were irrelevant.[274]

Then, after claiming the "serial killer" theory to be "entirely possible," Shafer concluded "the true problem with this situation is the lack of investigative experience beyond coming to the conclusion that these were all drunken mistakes." Ironically, since the college student had zero criminal investigative experience, Shafer's bashing of the La Crosse Police Department and the Wisconsin Department of Criminal Investigation was — no pun intended — dead wrong.[275]

Nonetheless, misinformation, especially in the age of social media, can create the perception of a scandal where none exists. And nothing gets a politician's attention more than a public hue and cry, even if the sentiment is based on a false premise. Just two weeks after Homan's death, the City of La Crosse's Alcohol Oversight Committee announced a public meeting in the aftermath of yet another Mississippi River alcohol-fueled drowning death.[276]

"We need to help young people understand that this truly is a community problem," said Alderwoman Rosemary Boesen, "and how important it is to take care of each other and be responsible." The committee meeting, Boesen explained, was organized to gather input from the public and to "clear up any misconceptions" related to the drowning deaths.[277]

At the meeting, public opinion appeared to favor the serial killer theory and/or took issue with the police department's handling of the investigations. Seeking to reassure the public, the La Crosse Police Department requested that the FBI "review" the drowning deaths of eight men. "We continue to stand by our findings," said La Crosse PD Lieutenant Dan Berndt. "There have been significant levels of alcohol involved in every one of these incidents and they are not related."[278]

For those unfamiliar with law enforcement jargon, a "review" is not a reinvestigation. During the review process, an outside agency reads the investigating agency's police reports to ensure acceptable protocols were followed while probing an offense. If an outside agency locates deficiencies, recommendations will be made to ensure a complete and thorough investigation.

Believing an FBI review of the La Crosse drownings would finally put the serial killer theory to rest, a report from the Twin Cities instantly revived the urban myth. At a November 21, 2006, news conference, Minneapolis Police Chief Timothy Dolan told the local media his department had "made an assumption" regarding Christopher Jenkins' death "and for that, for the Minneapolis Police Department, I want to apologize to the Jenkins family."[279]

"A source brought me a rumor," said Sergeant Pete Jackson, as he explained the Minneapolis PD's about-face. "Just a faint rumor of something that he had heard [in the county jail]." The information later led to an "eyewitness/suspect," who provided "specific details of the exact spot where Christopher Jenkins was thrown off the bridge."[280]

Nine months after the news conference, however, the Jenkins investigation was sent to the Hennepin County Attorney's office for a charging conference. After reviewing the matter, officials declined to file criminal charges and referred the case back to the Minneapolis PD for further investigation.[281]

Believing the Minneapolis police had swept the case under the proverbial carpet, the Jenkins family lashed out. "A police officer was involved with getting Chris kicked out of the bar, day one," said Steve Jenkins, the father of the deceased student, "and he has never been questioned by the Minneapolis Police Department. We have a problem with that. Anybody in that bar has never been questioned, we have a problem with that."[282]

Chuck Loesch, the private investigator retained by the Jenkins family, also took issue with the suspect's statement. The location on the bridge where the alleged crime occurred was, from an investigative perspective, somewhat problematic. The purported murder would have likely been observed by a witness on the heavily-trafficked, well-lit bridge that is blanketed with surveillance cameras. Tossing Jenkins over the side of the bridge would require the suspect to lift the grown student over a security railing and throw him five feet beyond the bridge support beam.[283]

After examining the serial killer theory in its totality, the Center for Homicide Research (CHR) reported Jenkins, as well as several other drowning victims, exhibited no signs of bodily trauma. "The Christopher Jenkins family alleges that their son was driven around the city for hours while he was tortured," a 2010 white paper from the respected nonprofit noted. "Torture tends to leave signs of trauma. There was no physical trauma identified in this case consistent with an assault."[284]

Researchers at the CHR further reported "confessions from correctional inmates are unreliable," in part, because twelve percent of prisoners "make voluntary false confessions." Many of these bogus confessions are made "in an effort to obtain social status or notoriety" within an institutional setting. Nevertheless, the Minneapolis PD's apology to the Jenkins family resuscitated the theory a killer was responsible for the drowning deaths.[285]

Ten months later, the feds weighed in. On the first day of the university's fall semester, the FBI's National Center for Analysis of Violent Crimes found "no evidence to support the serial killer theory." The center's report further indicated eight additional men had survived falls into the river while having "no contact with anyone else." The *Associated Press* seemingly poked fun at serial killer theorists by proclaiming there is "no bogeyman lurking in college-area bars."[286]

UW - La Crosse Dean of Students Paula Knutson told the press that — with no killer to blame — students may finally take responsibility for their actions when they abuse alcohol. "This report will help students," said Knutson. "There was doubt in their mind, which removed a sense of accountability."[287]

Still, as sure as alcohol would be served at La Crosse's next Oktoberfest celebration, the deaths would continue. The next tragic accidental drowning shattered the myths promulgated by Eugene Kane, the former racially focused columnist at the *Milwaukee Journal Sentinel.* "More than a few people I've discussed this issue with," wrote Kane in a 2013 column for *OnMilwaukee.com,* "insist the real problem is that drunken young white males go out on a bender and get separated from friends who apparently aren't looking out for them." Kane then asked " why black males who drink a lot don't end up in the river and why that particular racial angle seldom gets discussed." Had Kane conducted some basic research, he would have learned a twenty-four-year-old African-American man had drowned in La Crosse six years prior to his column being published.[288]

Unlike the vast majority of those who had perished in the waters in or around the Mississippi River, Christopher Melancon was not a college student, but a former U.S. Marine, a patriot, and an Iraq War veteran.[289]

On September 29, 2007, Melancon traveled from Bloomington, Minnesota, to La Crosse with Anthony Triplett. The two men had served in the Marines together, although Triplett had re-enlisted. Both planned to meet other friends in La Crosse during the city's annual Oktoberfest celebration. After arriving in town at about 12:30 p.m., they drove to the home of Carolyn Onopa. At about 2 p.m., Melancon and Triplett began drinking and later traveled to the city's downtown entertainment district.[290]

Triplett and Melancon visited a handful of taverns, including Dell's bar, Coconut Joe's, and the Animal House. At 1o:30 p.m., the two men walked to Hooter's, where Melancon made telephone contact with another former Marine, who now played rugby for UW – La Crosse. According to Triplett, Melancon left Hooter's to meet his friend at an un-specified location.[291]

At about 10:45 p.m., Melancon completed the two-and-a-half block walk to the Animal House bar and met Troy Syrjanen and his girlfriend, Melissa. For more than two hours, the three socialized over drinks. When Troy and Melissa decided to leave, they asked Melancon if he needed a place to stay, but the visitor explained he was "already hooked-up for a place." When the couple left, Melancon stayed behind at the Animal House.[292]

At about 1:15 a.m., twenty-one-year-old Amber Jorgenson was walk-ing across the Cass Street Bridge to meet her ride home after drinking downtown. Suddenly, a man to her right appeared to leave the bridge and enter a slough that fed into the Pettibone Lagoon. When Jorgenson looked down thirty feet, the man appeared to be swimming, but quickly "gave up." She ran beneath the bridge, scaled a fence, and entered the wa-ter in search of the man. Jorgenson asked two people in the area to called 911, but the man in the water had disappeared.[293]

After being flagged down, an officer immediately went to the area beneath the Cass Street Bridge and saw Jorgenson in the water. When an-other officer arrived, they escorted Jorgenson to shore. The officers quick-ly procured a personal water craft and searched the water for about a half-hour, but were unable to locate the man. While waiting for a dive team, an officer detected a strong odor of intoxicants on Jorgenson's breath. A portable breath test indicated her BAC was 0.197.[294]

Forty-five minutes later, a fire department dive team located the body of a black male at the bottom of seventeen feet of water on the east end of the slough. Once on shore, an officer observed the drowning victim had "a large amount of vomit in his mouth and nose." Firefighters unsuccess-fully attempted to revive the man for over ten minutes, at which time a medical doctor declared him deceased. An officer removed a wallet from the victim's pants and located Christopher Melancon's Wisconsin driv-er's license and seventy dollars.[295]

La Crosse police contacted Onalaska Police Officer Mark Moen and requested the assistance of his bloodhound, Clyde. Beginning at the Ani-mal House bar, the dog went south and sought to enter the front door of Hooter's. Clyde followed a scent trail to the Cass Street Bridge in the southbound lane of traffic. The dog crossed the roadway and stepped onto the sidewalk along the northbound side of the bridge. The scent ended at the location where Melancon left the bridge and fell into the slough, approximately ten blocks from the Animal House bar.[296]

The following day, the war veteran's corpse was taken from the St. Francis morgue to Hastings, Minnesota, for an autopsy. No signs of trauma were observed on the deceased. A toxicology test put Melancon's BAC at 0.24. Though a La Crosse PD investigator noted the investigation would continue, an "exceptional clearance" was filed on October 1.[297]

La Crosse Police Chief Edward Kondracki told the press a witness saw Melancon fall from the bridge but did not know if he tripped over the forty-two inch pedestrian railing or sought to commit suicide. "We'll never know what was in Christopher's mind at the time he went over the railing."[298]

Located on the opposite side of the Badger State, *Milwaukee Journal Sentinel* reporter Meg Jones observed that for "the second year in a row" someone who had formerly resided in the metro Milwaukee area had "drowned during the Oktoberfest weekend" in La Crosse — the first being Homan, and now Melancon, who was raised on the city's northwest side and graduated from James Madison High School in 2001.[299]

Unfortunately, Christopher Melancon's senseless death is steeped in irony. The former U.S. Marine had survived a tour of duty in war-torn Iraq, a place where improvised explosive devices maimed and killed American troops, only to lose his life to a colorless and odorless villain after socializing with fellow veterans in a relatively peaceful college town.

CHAPTER NINE

CHANGE OF VENUE

Some individuals — typically columnists or bloggers, particularly those who double as armchair cops — have bought into various myths regarding the strange deaths of young Wisconsin men. The last chapter debunked a fable peddled by Eugene Kane, who assumed, without checking, that only white men had drowned in La Crosse. Another myth, seemingly perpetuated by fans of television police procedurals, is that each of these victims met their demise in hard-drinking college towns.

One such individual is Vance Jones. "As an avid true crime buff," Jones blogged, "I had spent nearly two decades following court cases on T.V. and in newspapers — then crime truly hit home. In January of 2003, my brother Tommy was shot and killed by a group of unknown assassins."[300]

In his spare time, Jones has reviewed the "student-drowning cases" and believes these deaths are more than mere coincidences. "Missing college students are turning up dead. Either a serial killer is on the loose in the Upper Midwest, leaving victims in area rivers — or the Heartland is drowning in coincidence."[301]

In reality, these investigations are bound together by chemistry, not coincidence. While the circumstances surrounding "student-drowning cases" are, in many instances, bizarre, three members of the periodic table are generally present: carbon, hydrogen, and oxygen, the elements that comprise ethanol and water. When coupled with binge drinking, a small body of water or an exposure to the elements can be deadly.

Ira Hayes is buried in section 34, plot 479A at Arlington National Cemetery. During one of the bloodiest battles of World War II, Corporal Hayes' image, along with five other U.S. Marines, was captured in an iconic photo raising the American flag over the Pacific island of Iwo Jima. His bravery and fame aside, Hayes suffered from acute alcoholism. By the latter part of 1953, he had been jailed forty-two times on drunk and disorderly charges. Two years later, the thirty-two-year-old Hayes was found dead in an Arizona cotton field. In a ballad memorializing his life, legendary country singer Johnny Cash proclaimed that "two inches of water and a lonely ditch was a grave for Ira Hayes." However, at least two newspapers reported Hayes actually died from "exposure in the freezing weather and an over-consumption of alcohol."[302]

Ira Hayes was not a college student and his death did not occur anywhere near a college town. The law enforcement officers who frequently jailed the war hero may have referred to him as a hell raiser, a term that arguably could apply to Mosinee, Wisconsin native Jeffrey Liepitz. Just twenty-five miles north of the University of Wisconsin – Stevens Point, Mosinee is the antithesis of a college town and Liepitz was the polar opposite of a studious academic. Between March 1993 and September 2007, the troubled man was twice convicted of intoxicated driving. He was further charged with seven additional crimes, including marijuana possession (the case was reduced from a felony to a misdemeanor during plea negotiations). In early 2008, Liepitz and his thirty-four-year-old wife separated and he moved into his mother's Owen Street home. A fortune-teller did not need a crystal ball to predict 2008 was going to be a tough year for the heavily tattooed Liepitz.[303]

The path to Liepitz's demise began in mid-January 2008 when a local man, Blaine Kennedy, had property taken from his car. A rumor circulated a possible suspect was David Gresen, a close friend of Liepitz's. Several days later, Kennedy confronted Gresen and asked if he was "involved in taking items" from his vehicle. According to Kennedy, Gresen refused to answer and took a seat at the opposite side of the bar.[304]

In the early morning hours of February 10, Kennedy stopped at Dinger's, a sports pub located on 2nd and Main Streets. Within a matter of minutes, Gresen and "his friends," including Liepitz, arrived at the bar. As he selected songs from the jukebox, Kennedy was approached by Gresen, who asked if "everything was good." Kennedy replied "yes."[305]

Kennedy then went to the restroom. When he exited, Lieptiz approached him and said he was offered $20 to "kick his ass." Gresen then walked over and dumped the contents of a beer onto Kennedy's head. Bar patron Amber Stanley looked on as Gresen threw the empty beer bottle at the tavern's register. Gresen approached Kennedy, who was temporarily blinded by the beer, and Sara Eberhardy, who had stepped in front of Gresen. Stanley also intervened and grabbed Gresen around the shoulder. When Gresen tripped and fell to the floor, the fight was on.[306]

Being pulled from the pile, Gresen exited the tavern. When he tried to reenter, Kennedy stood in his way. When Kennedy turned to glance inside the bar, he was punched by Gresen. Standing near the door, Liepitz shouted, "You guys messed with the wrong fucking crowd," and left the bar with his friends.[307]

At 1:50 a.m, a dispatcher sent Mosinee Police Officer Tim Westergard to the fight at Dinger's bar. When he arrived on the scene, the officer observed four men walking on 2nd Street. A male in a tan colored jacket, later identified as Liepitz, entered an alley between 2nd and 3rd Streets and ran north towards Main Street.[308]

While interviewing Gresen, Steve McCabe, and Bradley Williams, officers were approached by Marlyne Rayome, who explained she had heard that her son, Jeff Liepitz, had been punched in the head during a fight. The officers told Rayome her son had fled the scene on foot.[309]

Two-and-a-half hours later, Rayome contacted the Mosinee Police Department to report Liepitz missing. Although she believed Jeff was not suicidal, Rayome told an officer her son had recently been served with divorce papers and was taking morphine for a back aliment. A Mosinee police officer conducted an extensive check of businesses and vehicles from Pine to Main Streets, and from 2nd to 4th Streets, but found no signs of Liepitz.[310]

On Monday, with Liepitz still missing, investigators contacted Gresen, who said that, prior to the disturbance, the missing man had consumed five to ten beers in a two hour span, but was not incapacitated.[311]

Investigators again canvassed the area near Dinger's and spoke with Hodges Place tavern owner, Mike Marquard. Marquard said Liepitz, Gresen, McCabe, and Williams had visited Hodges Place on the night in question and left between 1–1:30 a.m. When McCabe began making strange gestures to another customer, Marquard asked the men to leave. The tavern owner described Liepitz as being "quite mellow" and noted he had observed Jeff "much worse in past contacts while at the bar."[312]

Fearing the worst, officers requested the assistance of Jody Disher, a canine handler from JL & Rib Mountain Bloodhounds. Using a scent obtain from one of Liepitz's shoes, Disher used two bloodhounds to conduct two separate and distinct searches. Each dog tracked the missing man's scent from Dinger's bar to the Wisconsin River, then east to Water and Buchanan Streets. Believing Liepitz may have attempted to cross the thin ice, Mosinee police requested the services of the Marathon County dive team. [313]

On February 13, the dive team searched a stretch of the river with a sonar scan and an underwater camera, but found no signs of Liepitz. Two days later, the dive team conducted a more extensive search of the Wisconsin River, and again were unable to locate the missing man.[314]

A week later, members of the missing man's family injected themselves into the investigation. On February 19, Liepitz's brother, Bryan, telephoned the Mosinee Police Department. "Agitated" and using profanity, Bryan Liepitz said the police had not done enough to locate his brother and threatened to file a lawsuit. Tracking down rumors, Bryan told an investigator that Brian Olson had observed his brother in Dinger's forty-five minutes after the fight. When Bryan confronted Olson, the pizza maker denied seeing Liepitz after the fight.[315]

Two days later, family members spoke with a reporter from WAOW in Wausau. The reporter contacted the Mosinee Police Department to confirm that vomit, possibly belonging to Liepitz, had been found on a snowmobile path and investigators had collected a sample for a DNA comparison. However, an officer told the reporter no such evidence was ever located.[316]

Prior to the end of February, a dive team conducted another search of the area along the Wisconsin River near Buchanan Street, but, again, did not find any signs of Liepitz. On March 3, Rayome told a journalist she believed her son had been murdered and Mosinee police "were not doing enough in the investigation."[317]

After another unsuccessful search of a Wisconsin River in mid-March, the Wausau Paper Corporation agreed to drain the "power canal." On March 17, Wausau Paper Mill employees opened a series of valves that enabled water to drain from the canal back into the river. Three-and-a-half hours later, an officer observed a body floating in the water near Little Bull Falls Island and Highway 153, about one-hundred-and-fifty feet from the shoreline and a block east of Dinger's bar.[318]

When the body was pulled from the river, the corpse was attired in the same clothing Liepitz wore on the morning he disappeared. A wallet, secured to a pair of blue jeans by a chain, contained the identification of the missing man.[319]

The following day, the remains were conveyed to VA Hospital in Madison for an autopsy, which was performed by Dr. Robert Corliss. Dental records confirmed the body was that of Liepitz. X-rays did not detect any bone fractures. The only injuries found on the body were bruises to both knees and a small abrasion to the chin, both of which are consistent with a fall through thin ice. The cause of death was determined to be an accidental fresh water drowning. A toxicology report showed Liepitz's BAC was 0.24 and that tetrahydrocannabinol (THC) — the active ingredient in marijuana — was also in his system.[320]

Investigators theorized Liepitz had attempted to elude police by traversing the icy river from the west shoreline to the east, where his mother's Owen Street home was located. Although the deceased man's mother, Marlyne Rayome, told the press that the discovery of the body "brought relief and closure to the family," the rumor that Liepitz was murdered was proved incorrect.[321]

The Smiley Face Killer

Just six weeks after Mosinee police closed their missing person's investigation, the mainstream media reported that former NYPD detectives Gannon and Duarte believed a serial killer was "murdering dozens of male college students by making all the deaths look like accidents."[322]

"This is what we saw," Gannon told reporter Mike Celizic. "They're happy, as most serial killers are, and very content with their work and what they're doing and the fact that they're thwarting police."[323]

"This is a nationwide organization that revels in killing young men," said Dr. D. Lee Gilbertson, a professor of criminal justice at St. Cloud State University, whose statement to the press seemed to contradict his prior thoughts on the cases. During a January 8, 2007, visit to Eau Claire, police investigators offered Gilbertson access to their official reports and a detective gave a tour of the drowning scenes. At the conclusion of the visit, Gilbertson told an investigator "he thought our cases were most likely accidental drownings not related to the 'urban legend' theory."[324]

Having reviewed the drowning deaths in La Crosse, the FBI was skeptical. "To date, we have not developed any evidence to support links between these tragic deaths or any evidence substantiating the theory that these deaths are the work of a serial killer or killers," said a statement issued by the FBI. "The vast majority of these instances appear to be alcohol-related drowning."[325]

Regardless of what the FBI believed, the former NYPD detectives' "smiley face killer" theory caused at least one family to rethink the findings of the Eau Claire Police Department (ECPD). On April 30, 2008, the brother of drowning victim Josh Snell contacted an ECPD detective to explain he "had been working with two private investigators" and now believed the police had prevented him from challenging the findings of his brother's death. Although John Snell offered no new information, he alleged his brother's death was improperly investigated. In search of any new details, a detective telephoned Gannon, Duarte, and Gilbertson, but his calls were not returned.[326]

Shady Characters

To this point, an examination of strange deaths in the Badger State has debunked the following myths: That the victims were all white males; that the drownings occurred only in La Crosse or in other hard-drinking college towns; that the victims all had blood alcohol levels of over 0.20; and that those who lost their lives were all college-aged men. Although the death of Jesse Archer discredits three of the aforementioned urban legends, the Green Bay drowning investigation is suitable for a victim participation analysis.

Sometimes referred to as the "victim precipitation approach," adherents of victim participation theory believe some people place "themselves in harm's way through their own actions" and, therefore, give an offender an opportunity to target them. The model divides participants into two categories: passive and active victims. An example of a passive victim is an obviously intoxicated individual who, by his or her observable actions, is an easy mark for a robbery. An active participant is targeted by an offender while orchestrating or engaging in an illicit event (i.e. a drug dealer who is shot during a transaction with a supposed customer).[327]

On April 5, 2009, five-foot-five-inch, one hundred-and-fifty-five-pound Jesse James Archer drove his live-in girlfriend, Kimberly Stiles, to work at the Comfort Inn, two miles south of Lambeau Field. In the early afternoon, Archer met up with Jason Spindler. The two men had served prison time together at the Red Granite Correctional Center. After spending a few hours drinking at Mackinaws tavern, Archer purchased a twelve-pack of beer and, with Spindler in tow, drove twenty-six miles to Luxemburg, Wisconsin, to party at the home of a woman.[328]

At about 3 p.m., Stiles had finished work and called her boyfriend for a ride; however, Archer, who was partying hard in Luxemburg, "blew her off." Two hours later, Archer and Spindler arrived at the Comfort Inn and met Stiles, who immediately noticed her boyfriend had been drinking. Stiles told Archer to slide over to the passenger seat. She then drove the two men to Buster's, a tavern located on W. Mason Street. When Archer asked Stiles to come inside the bar, the couple began to argue. Archer agreed to leave after he used the restroom.[329]

Once Archer left the car, Stiles alleged Spindler hinted the three could "make a lot of money," which she assumed involved selling drugs. Stiles allegedly told Spindler she did not want to become involved in drug trafficking. A short time later, Archer returned to the car and said he was staying at the bar with Spindler. Upset with her boyfriend, Stiles left the two men at Buster's and went to pick up the couple's child, who was at a friend's home in the Upper Peninsula of Michigan.[330]

Once inside the bar, the two men ordered a pizza. The bartender, Lori Van Essen, noticed Archer and Spindler were "already intoxicated." As Spindler occasionally nodded-off and placed his head on the bar, Archer repeatedly called Stiles from a tavern payphone. An hour-and-a-half later, after devouring the pizza and having a pitcher of beer, the two men left Buster's at 6:35 p.m. Van Essen thought she overheard Archer say Stiles was going to give him a ride.[331]

The two men walked across the street to the Oneida Casino. Spindler told a detective that he began speaking with an acquaintance in the lobby and Archer entered the casino proper. Spindler alleged he never entered the casino and left without speaking to Archer.[332]

While at the casino, Archer called Stiles and purported to have won $1,100. He asked Stiles to retrieve his ID so he could claim the winnings. Stiles did not believe Jesse had "won any money" and, instead, believed her boyfriend had employed a ruse to convince her to return to Green

Bay.[333]

At about 9:30 p.m., Archer called from the Oneida One Stop, a convenience store one block east of the casino. He began screaming at his girlfriend to return to Green Bay and "drive him somewhere to spend the night." Stiles declined and told Archer he should call her in the morning.[334]

When Jesse had yet to call by the following evening, Stiles surmised something might be amiss. She telephoned Archer's mother, Susan, at her residence in Florida. Susan had not heard from her son and believed he was "probably just getting drunk or high and would eventually call." Susan told Stiles that Archer "always" calls on her birthday. If he failed to do so, that would be cause for concern. On April 20, fifteen days after Jesse Archer had disappeared, Susan Archer telephoned the Green Bay Police Department and reported her son missing.[335]

For the next four days, investigators did little to track the whereabouts of the missing man. Then, on April 24 at about 3 p.m., sixty-year-old Glenn Spevacek trekked across the Walnut Street Bridge en route to the Titletown Brewery. As he stood on the bridge "admiring" a nearby tugboat, Spevacek observed "a basketball" floating in the river. Upon closer examination, the object appeared to have "ears" and appeared to be "a human head."[336]

Within a matter of minutes, Green Bay police arrived on the scene and saw the body rapidly floating toward the Bay of Green Bay. Personnel from the fire department's search and rescue team eventually caught up to the corpse on the north side of the Dousman Street Bridge. After retrieving Jesse Archer's missing report, investigators located several distinct tattoos — a Grinch on his upper right arm, the name "Jesse" on his right forearm, and "James" on his left forearm — and determined the deceased was Archer. The body was clad in blue jeans; a black leather jacket; a black, short sleeve t-shirt; and black, yellow, and white Air Jordan shoes.[337]

After Archer's corpse was conveyed to the morgue, Kimberly Stiles telephoned the Green Bay Police Department. Stiles said she had been contacted by Susan Archer, who had received a death notification from the medical examiner. When asked if her boyfriend had any enemies, Stiles reported three men had recently "showed up" at her babysitter's home in search of Archer. The men said they were "old friends" of Archer and traveled from Sturgeon Bay. When the babysitter said he did not reside at the home, the men "implied" she was lying. Although they left "without incident," Stiles said Archer did not have any friends in Sturgeon Bay and "found this to be very suspicious."[338]

The following day, an autopsy was performed at the St. Vincent Hospital morgue by Dr. Mark Witeck. Documenting the autopsy, a detective reported no "significant injuries" were observed on Archer's body. However, another investigator, present at the river bank when the body was recovered, observed "blood coming from [Archer's] mouth and nose" and further noted the deceased had "a large mark on his forehead from an unknown cause" that resembled a five-to-six inch "backwards J." The area surrounding Archer's left eye "also appeared to have trauma." Archer was still in possession of a gold necklace and had $2.33 in his front pants pocket. The medical examiner later ruled the death a drowning. A toxicology report listed Archer's BAC at just 0.12, although prescription drugs — "within the normal parameters" — were also found in his system.[339]

Though the "backwards J" could be attributed to a passing boat prop, the injury could also have been caused by an iron, an object commonly found in hotel rooms. More troubling was the blood coming from Archer's mouth and nose, as well as the trauma around the deceased's left eye, which suggests some sort of blow to the face. Moreover, Archer's relatively low blood alcohol level resulted in a substantial gap in the investigation's timeline. Since Stiles and the bartender at Buster's observed Archer and Spindler were noticeably intoxicated, several hours would have passed prior to Archer's death. After all, by the time the two men left the bar at 6:35 p.m., they had been partying for almost six hours. In most human beings, alcohol typically metabolizes at a rate of 0.015 percent per hour. Had Archer achieved a BAC of 0.20 at the time he left Buster's, he would have drowned at around 11:30 p.m.[340]

One issue is the location of the body. At about 9:30 p.m., Archer telephoned Stiles from the Oneida One-Stop convenience store, located three-and-a-half miles from the Fox River. At the time of his death, Archer and Stiles were technically homeless. The couple stayed at area hotels until they ran out of money and management showed them the door. It is difficult to imagine a mildly intoxicated Archer simply roamed the streets for two hours. After Stiles made it clear she would not return to Green Bay, a reasonable investigator might surmise Archer contacted other friends in search of a ride and/or a place to spend the night.

Another critical piece of information was located in the video surveillance from Buster's, where Archer was seen wearing a long sleeve shirt. "The only thing noteworthy on the video [from the tavern] is that when we found Archer, he was not wearing the long sleeve shirt," a detective noted. "This would suggest that he took it off somewhere." People generally remove layers of clothing when they're too warm. The missing long sleeve search suggests Archer probably spent some time inside a well-heated apartment or a hotel room.[341]

Another piece of evidence was a text message mistakenly sent to the cell phone of a Green Bay firefighter. On April 25, at 1:10 p.m., the day after Archer's body was recovered from the Fox River, Thomas Malecki received the following message: "no, i didn't kill him, but he mayb [sic] killed himself they think. he was on the bar ph the whole time he was there w/broke up GF or wife – mom." Although it is unclear if Green Bay police ever identified the owner of the cell phone, the only people present at Buster's were Archer, Spindler, and the bartender.[342]

For the next two weeks, investigators sought to recreate the last few hours of Archer's life, but made little progress. Then, on May 2, a witness who had visited a makeshift memorial for Archer in Leicht Park reported he had been approached by four Native American men. One of men — described as tall, slender, and wearing his hair in a ponytail — identified himself as "Jason" and said Archer and he had used and sold drugs together. Jason alleged that Archer's girlfriend, Kimberly Stiles, "may have something to do with his death" because he had been present at their home when the couple had argued.[343]

Two days later, another witness called and offered information pertaining to Archer's and Stiles' whereabouts. The witness said the couple left Green Bay on April 2 to visit Stiles' brother in Michigan's Upper Peninsula. On April 4, the couple returned to Green Bay "with several types of drugs" and stayed at a local Motel 6. The following day, when Archer had not arrived to pick her up from work, Stiles called and asked if Archer had contacted the witness. A short time later, Stiles telephoned the witness again to report she had located Archer in Luxemburg, where Jesse went to purchase crack cocaine.[344]

On April 8, the witness received another call from Stiles, who reported she last saw Archer on April 5, after the couple "got in a fight." Stiles purportedly said Archer had "took off with a bunch of pills" the two planned to sell. The witness told an investigator "Kim" is much "bigger than Jesse," and the witness was present when Stiles had "physically assaulted" Archer in the past.[345]

As the probe into Archer's death continued, detectives had yet to resolve a problematic gap in the investigative timeline, this being the whereabouts of Jesse Archer from about 9:30 p.m. until his body entered the Fox River. Assuming that an open records request for police reports was fully completed, other additional steps could have been taken to eliminate some of these gaps.

If Archer had been a victim of foul play, the police reports suggest three parties had some sort of motive. One was Jason Spindler, a man two witnesses allege had trafficked drugs with Archer. The second person was Kimberly Stiles, who had several domestic spats with Archer and had argued with her boyfriend the day he disappeared. Finally, the three unidentified men who, while searching for Archer, mysteriously appeared at the home of Stiles' babysitter.

Having spent the better part of two months ascertaining his identify, investigators initially interviewed Spindler on June 24. The ex-convict provided a detailed and verifiable account of his whereabouts up to the time Archer and he arrived at the Oneida Casino. According to Spindler, he was unable to find a ride, walked home from the casino, and arrived around midnight. On the date he was interviewed, police reports note Spindler was contacted at his residence in Thorp, Wisconsin, a small town one hundred-and-fifty-two miles west of the casino. Although Spindler claimed to reside in Green Bay on April 5, his address is not noted in the police reports.[346]

After Spindler was "thanked" for "his cooperation," a detective did little to verify his statement. The easiest way to this would have been a check of surveillance video. Although detectives had the wherewithal to review the video from Buster's bar, they apparently declined to view the casino's surveillance footage. Casino's typically maintain a large bank of security cameras and store footage on servers for up to ten years. Certainly, any video footage that contradicted Spindler's statement would have sent up a red flag.[347]

A thorough investigation would further require detectives to pinpoint the location of Stiles. In possession of information from a witness that Stiles had previously roughed-up Archer, that her boyfriend had "took off with pills" the couple plan to sell, and that Archer and Stiles had been involved in a heated argument on the date he disappeared, confirming her whereabouts between 9:30 pm. to midnight on April 5 was paramount. Based on the police reports, Stiles voluntarily submitted her cell phone records. Although the individual telephone numbers are redacted, the last outgoing call was made from Stiles' number, assigned to a Green Bay local access and transport area (LATA), at 8:56 p.m. The last four incoming calls to Stiles' cell phone occurred between 9:30 and 9:53 p.m.[348]

Yet the incoming and outgoing telephone calls are one part of the total equation. When attempting to ascertain the whereabouts of a party, calls from a mobile device do not establish a party's location. Cellular telephones are registered to pre-determined LATAs, which appear on incoming and outgoing logs regardless of the party's actual location. The only way to pinpoint a cellular device's true position is to identify the cell tower accessed when the call was placed. Absent exigent circumstances, such as an abduction, a communications company usually requires a court authorized subpoena to retrieve such data. As it pertains to this investigation, it appears detectives relied on the call logs and did not seek a subpoena to determine the precise location of Stiles' mobile telephone.

A review of the police reports indicate Green Bay police did not corroborate Stiles' whereabouts with third parties. To do so, detectives could have contacted Stiles' babysitter in Michigan's Upper Peninsula and subpoenaed any credit or debit cards issued to Stiles. During a follow-up interview with Stiles, detectives could have asked detailed questions about her whereabouts, such as where she stopped for gas, and corroborated her statements through surveillance video or witness statements.

Two other missing pieces of the puzzle suggest that something was amiss on April 5: Archer's missing long sleeve shirt and the missing pills. The pills equated to money, and a reasonable investigator could conclude both Spindler and Stiles had a monetary interest in procuring the drugs. Neither the shirt nor the pills were ever found.

On the same date that an investigator "thanked Spindler for his cooperation," a Green Bay police lieutenant signed off on closing the case.

90

On July 21, absent a note from Archer or other creditable signs of ongoing mental health issues, a detective concluded: "This case is closed and has been ruled a Suicide/Accidental Drowning."[349]

Although the previous accidental drowning deaths of men in college towns were widely covered by the media, the strange death of Jesse James Archer — a case that is clearly suspicious and merits further investigation — received just a few paragraphs. In an article in the *Green Bay Press Gazette*, the Brown County medical examiner said Archer was "probably in the river several weeks" and "there were no immediate reasons to suspect foul play," unless, of course, he had carefully read through the police reports.[350]

CHAPTER TEN

UNDER THE WATER & IN THE WOODS

Wisconsin is home to nineteen major rivers and 15,000 lakes. The natural landscape explains, in part, why so many alcohol related drowning deaths have occurred in the Badger State. In other regions of the United States where bodies of water are few and far between, intoxicated men have also died. In the high desert of Gallup, New Mexico, hypothermia killed fourteen inebriated men during a six-month period that ended in April 2015. Although the national average for hypothermia deaths is 0.5 per 100,000 people, Gallup's rate of sixty-four deaths for every 100,000 during this period was one-hundred-and-twenty-eight times the national average.[351]

Gallup is not far from the Navajo Indian Reservation, where the tribe prohibits the sale of alcohol. Nonetheless, the city's gritty taverns serve those who venture into town. "One of the things that will never change in Gallup is the alcohol," said Native American Carl Smith, whose intoxicated son died from exposure. "The drinking, the liquor licenses aren't going away because they are how this city survives."[352]

Exposure deaths are rare when alcohol is removed from the equation, which makes the death of a Chippewa County, Wisconsin, man an abnormality. During the early evening of November 3, 2009, twenty-year-old Russell Plummer stopped at the Mornings Corner, a rural pub six and a-half miles west of Bloomer, Wisconsin. Plummer spoke with a friend, Tyler Girard, and discussed a possible trip to Atlanta with colleagues from the Army National Guard. He then left the bar, alone. Five days later, after missing a scheduled military drill, Plummer's mother, Penny Hetke, reported him missing.[353]

As the news of the disappearance spread, a married couple reported spotting a man driving a yellow car, similar to the Plummer's, on State Highway 178, thirteen miles east of the Mornings Corner. Investigators, however, were unable to confirm the driver's actual identity. Rumors swirled that an ex-girlfriend and her new boyfriend had suddenly fled to a neighboring state. The missing man's family suspected foul play.[354]

An avid hunter, Plummer frequented the Chippewa County forest, a vast area of woods and non-paved trails. This area's woodlands became the focus of an intense search. On November 10, a small group of Plummer's friends located his yellow Honda Civic on a logging trail three hundred and seventy-five yards west of Hay Meadow Flowage Trail, an isolated area a mile-and-a-half north of 225th Avenue. Investigators located the missing man's wallet and military identification inside the vehicle, which was parked at the top of a steep embankment. When an officer looked down the hill, he observed "a dark object" that seemed "out of place" near a swamp.[355]

As two sheriff's department investigators moved down the embankment, they located a box of Camel cigarettes and a water bottle. At the bottom, they found Plummer lying on his back and "deceased based on his appearance." The dead man's head was to the north, his right hand was "upright in the air," and his left hand was on the ground. The dead man's knees were "slightly bent" and tilted to the east. Movement from Plummer's feet had displaced leaves and made marks in the dirt surface. Small scratches were also observed on his forehead.[356]

The deceased man was attired in a green t-shirt, an insulated flannel shirt, blue jeans, and tan boots. The flannel shirt was unbuttoned and his pants were pulled down to the thighs. To the west of the body, a bare patch of dirt suggested "someone had stepped on and fell from some small tree branch." Marks in the dirt led investigators to believe Plummer slipped while constructing a shelter made of tree branches.[357]

On the evening Plummer went missing, the high temperature was 43 degrees. The following morning, however, the temperature dipped to 24. On the ground in the cold night air, and in some sort of distress, his body temperature decreased and hypothermia set in. When the coroner arrived, he pronounced Plummer dead at 4:15 p.m. The yellow Honda Civic was towed from the forest and secured in a storage facility.[358]

The following day, Plummer's corpse was taken to the Ramsey County, Minnesota, Medical Examiner's Office for an autopsy. Forensic pathologist, Dr. Michael McGee, found "no internal trauma and nothing extraordinary about the body." The external bruising and contusions were attributed to a likely thirty-eight-yard tumble down the embankment. McGee theorized an injury found on Plummer's left rib cage was a result of "marks due to clothing injuries, such as a zipper." A toxicology test indicated Plummer was sober when he died. The cause of death was listed as "probable exposure, fall, manner of death accidental."[359]

On November 12, an investigator examined the contents of Plummer's Honda, a car that could easily be classified as a "beater." Unsure how long the bucket of bolts would run, the owner declined to register the car with the Wisconsin Department of Transportation. The key to the Honda was in the ignition, the gear shifter was in neutral, and the car's battery was dead. In an effort to get the manual transmission car started, Plummer likely struggled to push the vehicle to an area where it would gain downhill momentum. Once the car began rolling, he could reenter and attempt to start the car. Sometime during this process, Plummer lost his footing, dropped his water bottle when he tumbled down the embankment, struck a tree, and bruised his ribs. The injured man likely descended to the bottom of the hill, where he sought to build a crude shelter. In the dark, he likely slipped on one of the branches, became disoriented and lost consciousness.[360]

There is one piece of evidence that casts some doubt on this otherwise solid theory: the deceased man's pants pulled down to thigh-level. After discovering the body at the bottom of the hill, an investigator noted the "pants [on the corpse] were wet." This piece of physical evidence could be explained by an unidentified head injury from either the tumble down the embankment or a secondary fall that impacted Plummer's ability to process information. [361]

"A closed brain injury," also known as a concussion, "is caused by a rapid forward or backward movement and shaking of the brain inside the bony skull that results in bruising and tearing of brain tissue and blood vessels." Closed brain injuries typically cause confusion in time and space, as well as a deficit in balance, which could explain the secondary fall. Another symptom is loss of bowel and bladder control. On the ground and unable to stand, Plummer may have sought to lower his pants to urinate.[362]

Investigators pinned their hopes on a forensic search of Plummer's pink Motorola Razor cellular telephone, which was found inside the Honda. The last outgoing text message was sent on October 31, and the available call data offered no new leads. Sheriff Jim Kowalczyk told the press Plummer had not accessed his "credit cards, ATM card or cell phone" after leaving the Mornings Corner pub.[363]

Four months later, investigators received information an eccentric local man claimed to have murdered Plummer. An extensive investigation showed bogus details were fed to the sheriff's department in an effort to "get back" at the alleged suspect for "a car sale that went bad." Still, Plummer's father, Jay North, believed his son was a victim of foul play and told investigators "he was not going away until he was satisfied whit [sic] what had happened." Although the family retained a private investigator, no additional information appeared to materialize.[364]

In November 2010, the deceased man's family shared its concerns with the public. "I understand he probably died of hypothermia," said Plummer's aunt, Peggy Stanford, "but hypothermia didn't put him at the bottom of that hill. That's the question, what put him at the bottom of the hill."[365]

"I was one of the first ones that thought this could've happened," Plummer's father told the press. "But as I got information from the sheriff's department, and photos of his injuries, I really started questioning it." North's concern was premised on a report the trees on the hill would have prevented his son's descent to the bottom. A more plausible explanation is Plummer was injured while tumbling down a portion of the embankment. Unable to climb the hill, he made his way to the bottom in an effort to establish a makeshift shelter.[366]

Two years later, the family held a meeting at the Cleveland Town Hall. North questioned the medical examiner's cause of death determination and asked the Chippewa County Sheriff's Department to reopen the investigation.[367]

"There are many cases when investigators are unable to determine the cause of death, therefore law enforcement personnel must rely on the Medical Examiner's autopsy results," said Sheriff Jim Kowalczyk. "The Chippewa County Sheriff's Department has no reason to dispute the findings of Doctor McGee of the Ramsey County Medical Examiner's Office." The sheriff further told the press there is "no evidence to support foul play" and his office would not reopen the case.[368]

From an investigative standpoint, it appeared Russell Plummer probably suffered an accidental death. His wallet was found inside the open car, which therefore ruled out robbery as a motive. Plummer's telephone records indicated he had no plans to meet another party in the forest.

One person with a possible motive was Plummer's ex-girlfriend, but she, along with her new boyfriend, had moved to Iowa prior to Plummer's disappearance. While a non-alcohol related exposure death is a statistical anomaly, it is very unlikely that a serial killer was lurking in the sparsely traveled Chippewa County forest on the lookout for an unsuspecting man to murder. At just five-foot-six, Russell Plummer was not a big man. He did, however, have significant military training and would have struggled if attacked.[369]

Deadly Shortcut

Two months after Plummer's death, an eighteen-year-old man went missing after attending a youth dance at the Stargate Nightclub in Superior, a city in the northwest corner of Wisconsin. A news release described Sylvester "Sly" McCurry, Jr., as a five-foot-ten, one-hundred-sixty pound "light skinned black male," attired in blue jeans and a gray fleece jacket.[370]

A senior at Duluth East High School, McCurry's family life had been challenging. When he was two years old, his father fled a courthouse after being convicted of attempted third degree criminal sexual misconduct. During his senior year in high school, McCurry moved away from his mother's home and resided with the family of his best friend, Keegan Couillard.[371]

On January 17, 2010, the two men told Keegan's parents they planned to attend a friend's birthday party. Instead, McCurry and Couillard crossed into Wisconsin and rented a room at the Superior Inn. By late afternoon, the two men began to drink, took a short nap, then left for the Stargate at 10 p.m. Once there, the two friends gradually separated as they chatted with their peers.[372]

Wisconsin Public Radio reported McCurry, who appeared intoxicated, was ejected from the Stargate's alcohol free dance at 11 p.m. He left through a rear door and was last seen standing in an alley by himself. Unable to locate his friend, Couillard assumed McCurry had returned to the Superior Inn.[373]

When the club closed around midnight, Couillard approached Angela Steegal and Tiffany Smith. Waiting on a ride home, the two sixteen-year-old girls were "pretty intoxicated" when Couillard invited them to his hotel room. The girls stayed at the room for about an hour and witnessed Couillard repeatedly "call McCurry over and over."[374]

Another witness told police she had heard McCurry "got into trouble with gangs" and rumors circulated a group "cut a hole in the ice and put McCurry's body through this hole." The skeptical witness told investigators no names were attached to the rumors and "no one actually saw this happen."[375]

Over the span of a week, investigators spent hours locating and viewing video surveillance footage. Twelve hours after the Stargate closed, Coulliard was observed entering a nearby convenience store with a suitcase in tow. McCurry did not appear in the video and a detective believed Coulliard exhibited no signs of "suspicious activity."[376]

Unable to raise his friend by telephone, Coulliard was under the impression McCurry's girlfriend may have given him a ride to the hospital to examine an injured finger. A day earlier, McCurry cut his finger while working as a cook. While at the Stargate, Coulliard noticed blood slowly seeping through the finger's bandage.[377]

On January 21, the police discontinued their search for McCurry. Investigators told the press they did not suspect foul play and "considered the possibility" the missing man "attempted to cross the St. Louis River harbor area in an attempt to get back to Duluth." A press release noted law enforcement had searched "the river, harbor, and piers in the area." Investigators clearly suspected McCurry had somehow entered the St. Louis River and drowned. However, the disappearance of another man in La Crosse once again fanned the flames of the so-called smiley face killer theory.[378]

Just three weeks later, twenty-one-year-old Craig Meyers disappeared after exiting his cousin's car in the 700 block of Market Street at 1:50 a.m. The Western Technical College criminal justice student had earlier attended a wedding reception and later patronized two downtown taverns. Jerrod Clements told investigators his cousin was intoxicated and Meyers "believed he was being dropped off at his girlfriend's residence."[379]

The following morning, Mark Meyers called the La Crosse Police Department to report his brother missing. Friends and family searched the downtown area for the missing man, who was last seen wearing a light green dress shirt, black slacks, black shoes, and a black leather jacket. Calls made to Meyers' cellular telephone went directly to voice mail.[380]

While checking a downtown location just north of the Courtyard by Marriott Hotel, an officer spotted an area "near a rocky ledge" adjacent to the Mississippi River, where it "appeared as if someone had been laying or sitting." There were, however, no footprints in the snow leading to this area, which caused the officer to believe "someone may have slid or rolled on this ledge." Staring downward, the officer saw "the outline of a human imprinted in the snow approximately six feet below the ledge," where a "clear outline of a head and a person's arms" were visible in the snow. From this spot, a set of footprints "lead away from shore" and headed north on the river. Twenty steps later, the footprints came to an abrupt end.[381]

The portion of the river where the footprints ceased was west of the intersection of King and Front Streets, just south of the Weber Center for the Performing Arts. From a high vantage point, detectives observed the footprints led to a spot on the Mississippi that was free of ice.[382]

On February 15, members of the La Crosse County Dive Team and the La Crosse Fire Department placed underwater cameras into the river where the footprints ended, but after six hours of searching, the efforts produced "negative results." The following day, the search resumed at 10 a.m. Five hours later, La Crosse Fire Captain Tom Wallerich's crew located a body. An hour-and-a-half later, divers removed a corpse from the water. Once on the gurney, investigators recovered a wallet from the deceased's right rear pants pocket, which contained Craig Meyers' Wisconsin driver's license. With the body recovered, detectives sought to piece together an investigative timeline.[383]

Advances in technology filled in some critical gaps. Retracing Meyers' probable route from the 700 block of Market Street to the intersection of King and Front Streets, a police sergeant observed two well-placed surveillance cameras at the Sara Lee Corporation. The company's plant manager, John Ryan, reviewed the video footage. He observed a man wearing a dark colored jacket, dark pants, and dress shoes, doing a "jumping jack-type hop-scotch-type maneuver" in the 400 block of Cass Street at 2:03 a.m. The white male then crossed the intersection of Fourth and Cass Streets and disappeared from view. After watching the video, an investigator wrote "this person is very similar to the description of Craig

Meyers."[384]

Using the Sara Lee location as a starting point, La Crosse County Deputy Sheriff Mark Moen responded to Fourth and Cass Streets with his trained canine, Daisy. After being offered a scent item of Meyers', the dog tracked west to an alley between Enterprise Rental Car and Pischke Motors, continuing north through the alley to King Street. Daisy then followed the scent west on King Street, past Front Street and to "the bank along the north side of the Courtyard by Marriott." When the dog reached the location where the footprints were located along the river bank, Moen discontinued the canine search "due to the bank being too steep."[385]

On February 18, Meyers' body was taken to the Minnesota Regional Medical Examiner's Office for an autopsy. The two-hour examination, performed by Dr. Susan Rowe, found no signs of trauma. A toxicology test placed Meyers' BAC at 0.28. La Crosse County Medical Examiner John Steers listed the cause of death as "cold water drowning with acute alcohol intoxication and hypothermia as contributing factors."[386]

In possession of the video tape, La Crosse police were certain the highly intoxicated Meyers tumbled from the river bank and — in the dark of the night — walked to and fell through the thin ice. The sole pair of footprints on the icy river showed the smiley face killer did not push the student into the water.

"From what I've seen," said the deceased student's father, Ken Meyers, "I have no inkling something else went on. From the dogs, the tracks in the snow, I think it was so cold that it just got the best of Craig and he couldn't function."[387]

Still, the strong physical evidence did little to dissuade smiley face killer theorists. Clearly irritated, La Crosse Police Chief Edward Kondracki did not mince words. "The previous river drownings have all been thoroughly investigated and re-investigated" by the Wisconsin Department of Justice and the FBI. "There is no serial killer! Police officers and River Watch volunteers have saved over fifty people in recent years who were either in the water, or on the edge of or attempting suicide in the river. Some cases are nearly identical to this one." Kondracki took further aim at the naysayers. "To rumor mongers: Please show some respect for the Meyers family   wild accusations of a rogue cop, long range hypnotists, and seductive female or smiley face gang are beyond the pale and demeaning to all."[388]

Three months later, as the harsh Superior, Wisconsin, winter finally ebbed, Robert Taylor, a security officer for the Midwest Energy Resource Company, saw something floating in the river about twenty-five feet from a major loading dock. The object slowly circled and came to a stop near a ramp. From the dock above, Taylor glanced down and saw a human body, clad in a dark striped shirt, floating on its back.[389]

Within a matter of minutes, officers arrived and photographed the body. The man was not wearing a jacket, but did have on a polo shirt. A pair of "sleeping shorts" covered the thighs. The flesh on the corpse's face "appeared to be missing" and a red band was attached to the left wrist. A company crane was used to transport the body from the water and onto the medical examiner's gurney. A wallet found in a pants pocket contained the Duluth East High School identification of Sylvester Mc-Curry.[390]

"It's over," McCurry's grandmother, Joan Durfee, told the press. "I guess we knew this may have been what happened. But it's hard. I don't know what we're feeling right now." Durfee also said her deceased grandson was wearing his same "Nikes and polo shirt" he had on the night he disappeared. "We don't know a whole lot more than that. They said they found him in the water down a street or an alley that would have been a route he left the Stargate."[391]

On May 24, McCurry's body was conveyed to the Anoka County, Minnesota, Medical Examiner's Office. The autopsy, performed by forensic pathologist Dr. Anne Bracy, took over four hours to complete. A full skeletal X-ray scan was taken and a bottle of Visine, a quarter, a Sony Ericsson cellular telephone, and a hotel key were detected in the deceased's left front pants pocket (at the time the body was recovered, the pants were down towards the ankles and remained in that position until the autopsy). Radiographs and an extensive internal examination found no bony or other internal injuries. Toxicology tests indicated McCurry's BAC was just 0.08, although the medical examiner explained the body's advanced state of decomposition may have naturally metabolized, lowering the blood alcohol result. After the exam, Dr. Bracy listed the cause of death as "undetermined" until the results of additional toxicology tests became available.[392]

While trying to retrace McCurry's steps, a break came for the investigators. Having heard the news pertaining to the recovery of the body, the deceased man's aunt, Jennifer Talbot, came forward to report that when she and her husband originally joined the search for McCurry, she observed footprints in the snow that came to an "end at the northwestern corner of Conner's Point," an area on a direct "incline downstream" from the docks of the Midwest Energy Company.[393]

Based on the new information, detectives theorized McCurry left the Stargate, returned to the hotel, and walked north to cross the river to Duluth. At some point, he fell through the ice. The river along the northwestern corner of Conner's Point contained "a large amount of large, underwater timbers," which hindered a sonar search of the area. The cold water temperature contributed to the buildup of decomposition gases, which caused McCurry's body to remain at the bottom of the river.[394]

In August, after the Superior Police Department received the final toxicology report, Douglas County Medical Examiner M.E. Witt determined Sylvester McCurry's death was due to "accidental drowning, likely due to cold water immersion and drowning."[395]

Once again, a team of investigators from two different law enforcement agencies dismissed the serial killer theory. McCurry's death also debunked Eugene Kane's report that all the men who had succumbed to alcohol-fueled drownings in the Badger State were white. Moreover, few people would classify Superior, a city that is home to a UW System campus with just 2,600 students, as a college town. Instead, the gritty municipality is better known for its large docks and shuttered rust belt industrial buildings.

CHAPTER ELEVEN

ON DRY LAND

For whatever reasons, bloggers and smiley face killer theorists tend to ignore peculiar dry land deaths. Although the circumstances that led to Russell Plummer's demise are unusual, online sleuths have yet to link his death to a serial killer. By excluding non-water related deaths, those who believe a serial killer is at large have hitched their trailers to the purported offender's signature — fresh water drownings.

Forensic psychologist Katherine Ramsland describes a signature as "an offender's method of perpetrating a crime" which "shows his or her degree (or lack) of planning, but some also leave a personal stamp that can reveal specific fantasy-driven rituals based on needs or compulsions."[396]

Like most of us, criminal offenders learn from experience. "A serial killer will alter and refine his MO to accommodate new circumstances or to incorporate new skills and information," notes Criminology Professor Scott Bonn. "For example, instead of using rope to tie up a victim, the offender may learn it is easier and more effective to bring handcuffs to the crime scene."[397]

Would it, therefore, be unreasonable to conclude that if such an offender actually existed, the smiley face killer may have altered his or her modus operandi by killing on land? After all, if those who died on land went missing after drinking in college towns, their deaths would match two of the criteria. Besides examining the third element, the manner and cause of death, another critical component is an individual's state of mind at the time of their disappearance. The probe of a missing Madison, Wisconsin, man is a prime example.

Joseph Sjoberg failed to report for work at Epic System on November 29, 2010. Two days later, his roommate reported him missing. A native of Seattle, Sjoberg owned a gray 1991 Chevrolet Caprice with Washington license plates. Detective Claire McCoy checked the missing man's cellular telephone records. Although Sjoberg had previously exhibited no interest in firearms, McCoy saw he had contacted an area gun store. Using the computer recovery program ENCASE, investigators learned Sjoberg had searched the Internet for ways "to make bombs and blow up vehicles." Police also obtained video from a gas station that showed Sjoberg buying a gas can and a lighter. The Madison Police Department then entered an attempt to locate/missing persons alert into the National Crime Information Center (NCIC) computer system.[398]

A few weeks later, Detective McCoy sought to locate Sjoberg through his cellular telephone. To find a device, a process known as triangulation is used to determine the user's last known location. When a cellular telephone is powered up, the device searches for a five digit System Identification Code. The telephone then transmits this code to the nearest tower, which identifies the nine digit telephone number, its owner, and the service provider. These numbers are automatically transmitted to local cell towers in an effort to find the best signal. This process occurs even when a cellular telephone is idle. By continuously searching the three nearest towers, law enforcement is able to "track the movements of the target phone" and locate the person using the device. In urban areas with a plethora of towers, law enforcement can determine the user's location to within a mile. Triangulation is not as accurate in rural areas, where fewer cell towers place the user within a ten to twenty mile radius.[399]

Eight weeks after Sjoberg vanished, Madison police told the press they believed the missing man was "in the area of Seven Hills Road and Maiden Lane in rural Dodge County," ten miles east of Columbus, Wisconsin. It is unclear if this location was determined by triangulation or the nearest cellular tower. Sheriff's deputies in Dodge County checked the area, but did not locate Sjoberg or his vehicle. Nearby Columbia County Sheriff's deputies on patrol were also asked to be on the lookout for Sjoberg's Chevrolet Caprice.[400]

In the interim, Sjoberg's roommate sought the assistance from the social media site, Reddit. "Joe was last seen on the near east side of Madison, WI – Baldwin at Sherman [Streets] He has short (not very short) brown hair and greenish eyes. He had about three or four weeks worth of a beard last time I saw him. Maybe wearing a hoodie, maybe a ski jacket."[401]

"Check his bank account," an anonymous poster replied, "I swear I was behind a dude who looked just like that at a Speedway station yesterday on 13th and College Ave. in Milwaukee." Other users of the site offered to put up posters and promised to keep "a keen eye out" for the missing man who seemingly vanished without much of a trace.[402]

On March 28, 2011, a man clearing trees on a section of property he leased observed the charred remains of a vehicle in a field a quarter mile north of Highway 60 and Schaeffer Road, in Columbia County — eleven-and-a-half miles west of the last cellular tower trace. Donald Borde told investigators he had observed human remains in the car, which was not present when he last visited the property in November 2010.[403]

A sheriff's deputy observed ice and snow on the car "indicating that it had snowed since the vehicle had burned." On the ground, near the front of the vehicle, a scorched Washington State license plate was linked to a "missing & endangered" person's 1991 Chevrolet Caprice. Raccoon tracks on the "outside hood, door and trunk area" suggested the car had been in the field for several months. A set of car keys were found on the ground near the driver's side door.[404]

Inside the vehicle, investigators found the interior burned to the metal. The fire had burned so hot that portions of the glass windows literally melted. The visible human remains consisted of bones "from a section of vertebrae or a spinal column" and "hip bones." The charred vehicle was loaded onto a flatbed tow truck and conveyed to the Columbia Medical Examiner's evidence bay garage.[405]

The following day, investigators from the Columbia County Sheriff's Department, the Wisconsin Department of Criminal Investigation, and the Madison Police Department processed what was left of the burned vehicle. Any items deemed to be human remains were "carefully collected and placed on a sterile cloth." The body parts included a section of liver, a section of muscle and a bone sample from the left femur. A DNA sample from the remains was collected and sent to the Wisconsin State Crime Laboratory.[406]

Barring a misidentification of the remains, the evidence strongly supported a suicide determination. A March 30 call to the Columbia County Sheriff's office filled in a rather large gap in the investigative timeline. Near the end of November or at the very beginning of December 2010, a Columbus-area farmer, Thomas Schultz, was driving on Highway 60 when he saw "thick, black smoke" coming from the area where Sjoberg's car was recovered. Schultz found the seasonal timing of the fire "strange" and kept an eye on the fire for about an hour, deciding not to report the matter to authorities. Schultz told investigators the fire occurred after the annual gun deer hunting season.[407]

An April 13, 2011, letter from the Wisconsin State Crime Laboratory officially closed the case. DNA obtained from Sjoberg's toothbrush and electric razor were a match to the remains recovered from the charred vehicle.[408]

Absent Detective Claire McCoy's thorough investigation, conspiracy theorists could have alleged foul play. After all, Sjoberg did not leave a suicide note and, according to his roommate and other relatives, was not noticeably depressed. Sjoberg's call to the gun shop, his Internet searches, and the video from the gas station slammed the door shut.

A Step into the Abyss

Over the course of my career, I have come into contact with hundreds of highly intoxicated people. Some of the things they say and/or do make no logical sense. Last year, an intoxicated man in Toronto entered what he believed was a taxi cab as the driver was filling the vehicle with gas. The Ford Crown Victoria sedan was actually a police cruiser and the man had a warrant outstanding for his arrest. In Mesa, Arizona, a highly inebriated man somehow found his way outside the Sky Harbor Airport terminal and wandered onto a runway. Sometimes, though, decisions made in a fuzzy state of impairment can be fatal. [409]

On May 27, 2011, at 8:26 p.m., Mark Wegener used his cellular telephone's camera to snap a picture of a bottle of booze. From his college residence on Cottage Street, the University of Wisconsin – Whitewater junior and "a small group of friends were routinely drinking" before visiting the "Downstairs/Librewery." A short time later, Wegener left his flat to attend a party just two blocks east on Boone Court.[410]

Sometime after 1 a.m., Wegener told his friends he was leaving the party for home. Although he had been drinking, the student's friends believed he was "alert enough to walk home."[411]

For whatever reason, Wegener did not return home. Instead, he telephoned his employer, Ryan Kastner, who let the call go to voice mail. Finding it odd an employee would contact him in the wee hours of the morning, Kastner decided to return the call. When Wegener answered, he seemed confused, "thought he was speaking with someone else," and sounded as if he was trying to "catch up with someone" on foot. When Kastner asked his employee if he was "all right," Wegener finally realized he was speaking to his boss. "Everything is good, Ryan. Peace out."[412]

Several hours later, after calls made to his cellular telephone went directly to voice mail, Wegener's roommates pounded on his locked bedroom door, but received no response. Believing something was amiss, the men forced their way into the room "to find an empty bed." After making several calls to friends to check on Wegener's whereabouts, the roommates feared the worst and contacted the Whitewater Police Department.[413]

Initially, the Whitewater Police Department declined to list Wegener as a missing person; however, officers searched certain sections of the city and attempted to identify possible witnesses. In the interim, the missing man's roommates contacted his parents, Jeff and Sandy Wegener, of Hartland, Wisconsin. The couple was vacationing in Jamaica and immediately returned to Wisconsin. Wegener's friends and roommates combed the streets of Whitewater "desperately looking for any sign" of the missing man, but found nothing.[414]

Then, on the morning of May 30, an officer from the Whitewater Police Department ventured outside the city limits to search Whitewater Limestone, Inc.'s large quarry at 9074 S. Franklin Street. Beneath a seventy-foot bluff, the officer observed a white male lying on his back at the quarry's bottom. The body was adjacent to a washed pile of two-inch thick limestone. An hour earlier, the quarry's manager, Mike Merriner, had loaded some limestone from the pile into pick-up trucks, but did not see the body on the other side. The corpse was soon identified as Mark Wegener.[415]

At the top of the bluff, investigators attempted to trace the dead man's steps. North of the quarry, a large path beneath several power transmission lines offered easy access from Franklin Street. A series of thick bushes, which could not "be easily penetrated," ran along the quarry's northern edge. There was, however, a small gap in the shrubs which led to the steep bluff.[416]

Investigators found it odd Wegener would wander three miles south to the quarry. Two significant gaps made the investigative timeline problematic. The first was the forty-minute break from the time he left the party on Boone Court to the 1:40 a.m. telephone call he made to his employer. The second issue was Wegener's whereabouts after the call.

On May 31, Waukesha County Medical Examiner Dr. Lynda Beidrzycki conducted Wegener's autopsy and determined the twenty-year-old man had died of multiple fractures after falling seventy feet into the quarry. Wegener's BAC was just 0.106 — a level inconsistent with the confusion he exhibited during the telephone conversation with Ryan Kastner.[417]

Oddly, the police reports received through an open records request did not include the final coroner's report and toxicology results. As a result, one can only speculate about Wegener's whereabouts and activities after leaving the party on Boone Court. Clearly though, Kastner's statement suggests Wegener, regardless of what he told his friends, did not go home. Instead, he was walking about trying to catch up to someone.

On a Facebook page titled *UW-Whitewater Confessions*, a post from a purported friend of the deceased student warned others they should not walk home alone. "Whitewater is not as safe as it seems," wrote the poster. "The police were extremely unhelpful/uninterested" and ruled Wegener's death accidental "by default." Yet, one would believe such a shoddy investigation would draw protests from the Wegener family, who were privy to the details of the final toxicology report.[418]

One week after Wegener's autopsy, the Whitewater Police Department received an email "in regards to some vandalism." Found on the corner of Clark and Caine Streets, one-and-a-half miles from the quarry, was a spray painted smiley face. "There were also concerns," wrote the case detective, "that Wegener's death could be linked" to the Smiley Face Killer, classified as an "urban legend" by the Walworth County Sheriff's office.[419]

Although Wegener's fall at the quarry is rather bizarre, so was the intoxicated man wandering onto the airport runway in Phoenix. Still, one has to wonder why the student told his friends he was heading home when he clearly did not do so. Did he stop by someone's home to procure some type of mind-altering substance? If so, did he walk to the quarry or was he driven there by another party? Unfortunately, investigators in

Whitewater did not locate the technological evidence Detective McCoy had uncovered in Madison.

CHAPTER TWELVE
BACK TO SCHOOL

Most people with an Internet connection are familiar with the Darwin Awards, a project that recognizes individuals whose poor decisions result in their immediate deaths. The passing of one person, thirty-year-old Matthew Zeno, led me to wonder how many men have died trying to urinate.

In early July 2013, Zeno and his twenty-six-year-old girlfriend left a Brooklyn, New York, bar. While waiting for the subway, the couple searched for a place to relieve themselves. Zeno descended to the train's tracks and, as he paused to open his zipper, came into contact with the third rail. He "was zapped with 625 volts of electricity" and died from a heart attack.[420]

Several anglers have also died while trying to relieve themselves. The Lifesaving Society advises boaters to "never stand up in your small powerboat, canoe or other similar watercraft" and reports "numerous drownings occur when fishermen stand up to urinate over the side of a boat."[421]

In several instances, alcohol was a contributing factor. When a New Zealand man decided to relieve himself near the side of his friend's boat, he fell overboard. Thrashing in the water, Paddy Rosson raised his hand for help. By the time his friend noticed something was awry and turned the boat around, Paddy was face down in the water. Rosson's BAC was "at least three times the legal alcohol limit for driving."[422]

In the Badger State, an inebriated young man, likely on the lookout for a place to relieve himself, was found floating in a river near Eau Claire's Water Street District.

On September 2, 2011, Joshua Lewis and James Zahn enjoyed what was left of summer by tubing on the Chippewa River. After the two men passed under the footbridge leading to UW – Eau Claire's lower campus, they spotted what they believed was a log in water. Lewis and Zahn maneuvered their tubes closer and saw "legs, shoes, shorts and a t-shirt." Zahn stayed with the body while Lewis went ashore, found an emergency alert box, and pushed the button to notify law enforcement.[423]

When police and EMS arrived, they found a male in his twenties floating face down in the river less than thirty feet from shore. The deceased was clad in a black St. Paul Harley-Davidson t-shirt, tan cargo shorts, black socks and one shoe on the right foot. Once the body was ashore at Hobbs landing, an assistant medical examiner searched the corpse and found a wallet in the right rear pants pocket. A Wisconsin driver's license identified the dead man as twenty-two-year-old Ricardo Gonzales. A cellular telephone, money and a plastic beer mug were also recovered. Investigators further observed the zipper "was down on his shorts."[424]

The following day, Dr. Robert Ridenour conducted an autopsy and observed no noticeable trauma to Gonzales' body. A preliminary blood test indicated the deceased student's BAC was 0.19.[425]

An Eau Claire native, Gonzales was a member of the university's wrestling team and resided on Graham Street with three other roommates. Over the summer months, however, those who boarded with Gonzales worked or traveled to their hometowns. One roommate, Brian Reier, was at this parent's home in Stillwater, Minnesota, where he trained with the National Guard. Reier recalled reading an August 31 Facebook post of Gonzales', which read, "Anybody have a mug club mug." Reier suggested investigators speak with John Ames, who was the deceased man's best friend.[426]

A few hours later, an investigator located Ames, who identified himself as an assistant UW – Eau Claire wrestling coach. Ames told police that on August 31, at about 4:30 p.m., he had arrived at Gonzales' Graham Street residence. A short time later, both men helped a mutual friend, John Bernstein, move furniture into his new apartment. Afterwards, Bernstein, Ames, and Gonzales went to Dooley's Pub on Water Street, where they ate dinner and shared two pitchers of beer. At about 7 p.m., the three men left the pub and went their separate ways.[427]

Ames returned home, rested, showered, and returned to Gonzales' residence, where they watched television and began drinking "quite a few" shots and beer. Sometime after 9 p.m., Matt Riechhoff stopped by and agreed to give Ames, Gonzales, and Bernstein a ride to Brother's Pub on Water Street. It was Mug Night at Brother's, where "the initial mug is $3.50, and refills cost $1 for domestic tap beers and $1.50 for rail drinks."[428]

For the next two hours, Ames and Gonzales slammed beers and shot pool. At 10:32 p.m., video surveillance showed the two men leaving Brother's Pub. They then walked a half block to The Pickle, a tavern on the southeast corner of Fourth and Water Streets. A noticeably intoxicated Gonzales dropped his ID at the door before entering.[429]

Once inside The Pickle, the two men socialized with another friend, Zach Weisenberger. Ames told an investigator "this is where the night got very fuzzy" and, due to an alcohol induced blackout, he did not recall seeing Gonzales inside or leaving the bar. The following morning, when Ames awoke, he checked his bank account and observed he had purchased food at Jim's Pizza, but had no memory of being at the restaurant. He assumed he simply walked home afterwards.[430]

While at The Pickle, Weisenberger noticed that Ames was "very intoxicated" but still took advantage of the two-for-the-price-of-one drink special. At about 12:20 a.m., Weisenberger combed the bar for Ames and Gonzales, but both men had left. Video surveillance depicted a "very intoxicated" Gonzales leaving The Pickle at 10:58 p.m., staggering into people as he walked eastbound on the sidewalk.[431]

In an effort to ascertain Gonzales' whereabouts, detectives obtained his cellular telephone records from Sprint. The last outgoing call was made at 10:15 p.m., prior to Gonzales and Ames leaving Brother's Pub. Investigators later learned a nineteen-year-old woman had sent a text message to Gonzales at 11:16 p.m. stating, "Ricky, I'm not banging Stevie." When she did not receive a reply, the woman sent another text message at 11:27 p.m. and proposed a sexual liaison. Gonzales never replied to her text messages and the woman told investigators she had not heard from him since.[432]

Absent any information concerning the deceased man's whereabouts, investigators had exhausted all leads. One theory is an intoxicated Gonzales staggered to a bike trail adjacent to the Chippewa River. In an effort to conceal himself from public view while urinating, Gonzales entered a wooded area that separates the path from the water. After unzipping his pants, Gonzales slipped and fell face first into the river.

Slippery Slope

Two months after the Eau Claire Police Department had concluded its probe of Ricardo Gonzales' death, another man drowned just sixty-five miles to the west near the small town of New Richmond, Wisconsin.

On December 6, 2011, at 6:30 a.m., a St. Croix County deputy sheriff was dispatched to "a one vehicle crash" on County Highway K near County Highway T. When he arrived, the deputy found a blue 2000 Chevrolet Malibu rolled over onto the driver's side of the vehicle. "I could see the vehicle had been eastbound on Co. Rd. K," the deputy noted, "and was going around a slight curve." The car then deviated onto the road's shoulder. When the driver overcorrected, the Chevrolet crossed the centerline, left the road, entered a ditch, and rolled over.[433]

Looking inside the car, the deputy noticed three spots of blood on a door post. It appeared the driver, who had been trapped inside the car, kicked out the windshield. Footprints in the snow tracked to the east for about twenty yards, then migrated to the road's north shoulder. The driver again walked eastbound for a short distance before the footprints stopped.[434]

The vehicle listed to Joseph Gillis of New Richmond. Unable to contact the car's owner by telephone, the deputy drove to a home on Highway 64. Once there, Joseph Gillis told the deputy his twenty-two-year-old son, Jeremy, was using the Chevrolet. In an effort to locate the injured party, the deputy contacted area hospitals, but none had admitted Gillis.[435]

Concerned for Jeremy's welfare, members of the Gillis family responded to the scene of the crash and began searching the area. At about 9 p.m., the family called the sheriff's department to report a fresh set of footprints that led down a hill from a park-and-ride lot. At the bottom, they found Jeremy Gillis floating in the Willow River.[436]

When a deputy arrived, he observed a male, later identified as Jeremy's brother, Justin, in the water pulling what appeared to be a drowning victim and shouting Jeremy's name. The deputy assisted by lifting the body ashore, but could not locate a pulse. Gillis' body was cool to the touch. At 9:31 a.m., the medical examiner was summoned to the scene and pronounced Jeremy Gillis dead.[437]

Retracing the deceased man's footprints, a crime scene investigator found marks in the snow where Gillis had apparently slid down the hill from the park-and-ride lot and tumbled into the Willow River. The only mark found on the body was a small, non-life-threatening cut above Gillis' right ear. Detectives theorized Gillis had tumbled down the hill, struck his head, fell into the cold water, and succumbed to hypothermia.[438]

Content with the investigation's findings, the Gillis family did not request an autopsy. Yet a report from the Wisconsin State Laboratory of Hygiene shed some light on the underlying cause for Jeremy Gillis' driving and disorientation: The dead man's BAC was 0.238.[439]

A serial killer played no role in the tragic death of Jeremy Gillis. Instead, the twenty-two-year-old man, who had recently fathered a child and entered into a judgment for child support, met his demise in an attempt to avoid a civil forfeiture intoxicated driving charge.[440]

Deadly Shortcut

With Gonzales' and Gillis' deaths in the news, one would think friends would stick together, especially when an out-of-town guest is visiting. Even in the era of social media, attention spans are short. Just thirty-two days after Justin Gillis fished his brother's corpse from the Willow River, tragedy struck again.

On January 7, 2012, twenty-one-year-old Ripon College student Michael Philbin arrived in Oshkosh, Wisconsin, around 8 p.m. After parking his Toyota Prius in a driveway at 619 Frederick Street, Philbin walked about a mile to a home at Wisconsin and Scott Streets. Once there, he met up with two friends, Eric McCullen and Brielle Londre, at a birthday party.[441]

The party broke up before midnight and those in attendance agreed to meet at Kelly's, a bar just six blocks away. Nineteen-year-old Katerina Novakova met Philbin at the party and requested that he walk with her to a friend's home on Pearl Street. When the two arrived, Novakova's friend was not home. They then walked a few blocks to Topper's Pizza, where Philbin ordered a pizza. Novakova remained at the restaurant for fifteen minutes, but left before the pizza was done.[442]

With the pizza in tow, Philbin crossed the street to Kelly's Bar and continued drinking. At about 12:30 a.m., McCullen and Landre left Kelly's for Polito's, a pizza joint around the corner on High Avenue. Philbin chose to stay at Kelly's with the group from the birthday party.[443]

At 12:45 a.m., Londre received a text message from a friend stating the group from the party was moving to Molly McGuire's, a tavern just two blocks away on Campus Place. McCullen and Landre assumed their friend had followed the crowd to Molly McGuire's. Instead, Philbin remained at Kelly's and continued drinking.[444]

At 1:23 a.m., Philbin exited Kelly's and entered a parking lot to the east. Two minutes later, he reentered the tavern. At 1:42 a.m., bar bouncer Alex Kessner told a colleague, Keith McLeod, that a group of women reported Philbin was annoying them. A short time later, Kessner approached the intoxicated student and told him to "socialize with other individuals." At 1:55 a.m., a woman from the same group approached Kessner and complained that Philbin had "tried to stick money" in the rear pocket of her blue jean pants. The bouncer again approached the drunken man, discussed the allegation, and escorted Philbin out the tavern's north side door. At 1:58 a.m., surveillance video showed him walking north through the parking lot.[445]

When detectives viewed the surveillance video from Kelly's Bar, they further observed Philbin stumble and take a seat at the bar by himself. Besides the two "annoying" contacts with the group of women, the drunken gadfly "had very little contact with other persons."[446]

At 2:10 a.m., Eric McCullen's roommate, Cody Sinkula, received a text message from Philbin that read "Uh." Sinkula immediately telephoned to check on the caller's welfare. When asked if he needed directions to Frederick Street, Philbin reported he was "fine" and "knew how to get back to the house."[447]

Twenty-seven minutes later, Alex Jalovec, a security guard for Rockwell, heard someone yelling outside the window of a guard station adjacent to the Fox River. Initially, Jalovec thought "it was some college kids in the area yelling and talking loud." When the yelling continued, the security guard grabbed a flashlight and went outside to investigate. Scanning the river with the flashlight's beam, Jalovec saw "a head and either a hand or a foot sticking out of the water." It appeared someone had fallen through the thin ice and he "could see there was a man struggling to stay above water." After calling 911, thirty seconds passed before the man "went under."[448]

With the missing student's father, Joe Philbin, being the Green Bay Packers' offense coordinator, news regarding the incident went national. With the Philbin's in Oshkosh, a dive team from the Winnebago County Sheriff's Department searched the river east of Rockwell Avenue. At about 3 p.m., an easily identifiable corpse was pulled from the icy river. A Motorola cellular telephone, a wallet with a Wisconsin driver's license, keys to the Toyota Prius, and two lighters were recovered from the body.[449]

The deceased's clothing had no tears or other damage. The only visible injury to the body was a small cut on Philbin's nose, likely caused by the fall through the ice. The body was transported to Madison for an autopsy. A full examination of the corpse showed no signs of an assault or foul play. In March, a toxicology screen listed Philbin's BAC at 0.176. Marijuana was also found in his system. As a result, Winnebago County Coroner Barry Busby listed the cause of death as accidental drowning.[450]

Once again, technology and a good eyewitness shot the smiley face killer theory to shreds. Still, friends, family, and investigators surely asked themselves why Michael Philbin would stagger onto the icy Fox River. Then again, why did the inebriated student try to place money in a woman's rear pants pocket? The answer is relatively simple: The actions of drunken people often make very little sense.

Birthday Splash

One of life's rites of passage is a young adult's twenty-first birthday. Millions of Americans celebrate this milestone by consuming copious amounts of alcohol. The consequences of such merriments are usually bad hangovers. Yet a study published in *The Journal of Consulting and Clinical Psychology* found "data from a sample of 2,518 college students suggest that 21st birthday drinking poses an extreme danger" and "12% of birthday drinkers (men and women) reported consuming 21 drinks." The authors of the study found it "imperative that investigators consider a variety of potential interventions to minimize the harm associated with this rite of passage."[451]

Four years after the published study, University of Wisconsin – Stevens Point student Eric Duffey celebrated his twenty-first birthday a few hours early. On March 2, 2012, at about 7 p.m., Duffey hosted a small gathering at his apartment, located at 728 Isadore Street, adjacent to the university's campus. Present at the gathering was Zachery Cleeman, who believed Duffey had consumed five or six beer prior to leaving the apartment a few minutes before midnight. Several friends, including Amanda Gauthier, Daniel Phillips, Katherine Gillis, and Alyssa Bruckner, accompanied Duffey on a walk downtown.[452]

When the clock struck midnight on March 3, Duffey and the others had completed the mile walk. The birthday boy downed his first legal drink at the Sugar Bar. A few minutes later, Duffey's girlfriend, Elly Keily, stopped at the tavern. Keily had an early morning class and stayed for just ten minutes.[453]

Within the span of a half hour, the party moved to four different taverns: Mug Shots, Elbow Room, Graffiti's, and Joe's. During this period, Duffey slammed five shots and two mixed drinks. At about 1 a.m., the student told his friends he was tired and was "going to head home." A friend, Steven Lenz, asked Duffey if he would like someone to accompany him home. Duffey said he was "fine," left Joe's Bar and walked towards Main Street.[454]

At 1:36 a.m., Duffey placed a cell phone call to Eric Anderson, a friend who was originally with the group, but stayed behind at Graffiti's. Duffey was attempting to contact Elly Keily. In an inebriated state, he had apparently entered the wrong telephone number. When Duffey realized he was speaking with Anderson, not his girlfriend, the "conversation ended pretty quickly."[455]

A short time later, Paul Schiller returned from work, stepped outside his Portage Street home to smoke a cigarette, and heard a male voice yelling, "Help, someone help!" The voice came from an area near the Clark Street Bridge, a two-block-long structure that crosses the Wisconsin River. Schiller reached for a flashlight and along with his dog, went to the area to investigate.[456]

Schiller made his way through Pfifner Park. Once south of the band shell, he walked the Green Circle Trail, a path abutting the eastern bank of the Wisconsin River. Schiller stood quietly on the trail for several minutes, but did not hear the voice or see anyone splashing in the water. After scanning the river with his flashlight, he walked the trail to the Clark Street Bridge. Schiller did not observe any footprints "walking out onto the ice." When his dog did not detect anything unusual in the area, he returned home and did not report the matter.[457]

At 2 a.m., Keily found it odd that her boyfriend did not sent a text message indicating he had arrived home safely. Over the course of the next two hours, she sent three text messages to Duffey, but he never replied. When Keily telephoned Duffey, the call went directly to voice mail.[458]

The following morning, Duffey's parents, Daren and Joan, arrived in Stevens Point from Verona, Wisconsin, to meet their son and a group of his friends for lunch. On the way, Joan had attempted to contact Eric to no avail. When the couple arrived at the Isadore Street apartment, their son's friends were present, but Eric was nowhere to be found. The missing student's Ford Explorer was in the apartment complex parking lot covered with snow.[459]

They Duffeys immediately reported the matter to the Stevens Point Police Department. Investigators contacted the missing man's cellular telephone provider and learned his last known location was probably within a one mile radius of 1100 Minnesota Avenue.[460]

Within an hour, administrator's at UW – Stevens Point put out a call for action. One hundred-and-fifty volunteers met at the Center Point Mall parking lot and were divided into seven groups. The expansive search yielded no signs of the missing student.[461]

With the foot search in progress, investigators caught a break. When Paul Schiller caught a glimpse of the visible police presence from the window of his Portage Street home, he told an officer he had heard a male yelling for help sometime after 1:30 a.m. As a result, law enforcement focused their efforts on "a water recovery operation" along the north side of the Clark Street Bridge.[462]

The river search was aided by "a local group of experienced, private divers" and began at 10:30 a.m. Two-and-a-half-hours later, diver Robert Butt located a body at the bottom of twenty feet of water fifty yards north of the bridge. Once ashore, the deceased was identified as Eric Duffey.[463]

Two days later, Portage County Coroner Scott Rifleman viewed the body during an autopsy in Madison. The only trauma found on the body were "minor abrasions consistent" with coming in "contact with the river bottom." The coroner further noted Duffey had on a water-saturated "down filled-type jacket" that made it "extremely difficult to remove himself from the river." Rifleman recovered a set of keys, twenty-two dollars in cash, and a wallet from Duffey's person, which ruled out a robbery motive. Toxicology results indicated the late student's BAC was 0.196. Duffey's vitreous eye fluid alcohol level was 0.22 and his urine was 0.312.[464]

Before clearing the case, detectives sought to close a gap on the investigative timeline by identifying Duffey's whereabouts from about 1 a.m. to the 1:36 a.m. cell phone call to Eric Anderson. Several taverns in the area — the Sugar Bar, Mug Shots, and Elbow Room — did not have surveillance systems. The Outfit Bar did have working cameras with two angles of the sidewalk; however, the footage, between 1 a.m. and 2 a.m., revealed no images of the student. After leaving Joe's Bar, Duffey likely stopped at one of the taverns without video surveillance. After the terse phone conversation with Anderson, the intoxicated student probably wandered onto the ice in the dark and fell into the cold river.[465]

A close friend of the deceased student, Chris Borgerding, offered another theory. Duffey was an avid environmentalist and may have " just went to stand by the river, just to be near it." UW – Stevens Point student Lizzy Schultz had known Duffey since grade school. "I'm surprised that he would end up alone in that kind of a situation." Like too many others celebrating their twenty-first birthdays, excessive alcohol consumption was the primary culprit.[466]

Psychedelic Plunge

Intelligent people are not necessarily thoughtful people. "Very bright individuals (with IQs above 125)," a *Psychology Today* report notes, "are roughly three-tenths of a standard deviation more likely to consume psychoactive drugs than very dull individuals (with IQs below 75)." The findings of the United Kingdom's *National Child Development Study* found a certain disconnect between bright children and common sense. "The fact that more intelligent individuals are more likely to consume alcohol, tobacco, and psychoactive drugs tampers this universally positive view of intelligence and intelligent individuals."[467]

The findings of the aforementioned study are consistent with the strange deaths of young men in the Badger State. After all, the vast majority of those who tragically died were college students with seemingly bright futures. In essence, one bad day preceded by a series of poor decisions, primarily lifestyles peppered with substances abuse, transformed these once vibrant individuals into actuarial statistics. The death of University of Wisconsin – Whitewater student Benjamin Fuder is a prime example.

On July 28, 2012, Fuder's parents, Brad and Chantal, appeared at Whitewater police headquarters to file a missing person's report. The couple explained their son had failed to report for work at 5 p.m. According to conversations with Benjamin's friends, he was last observed at 12:30 a.m. walking west on W. Whitewater Street. Officers and detectives began the process of piecing together an investigative timeline.[468]

On July 27 at 7:15 p.m., Ryan Peterson and Jeff Vogel, friends of Fuder's roommate, Michael Schildt, arrived in Whitewater. The two men and another friend, Josh Crawford, planned to attend a golf outing the following morning. While at the residence at 403 S. Janesville Street, the four men began "pre-gaming," a term used in reference to consuming alcohol prior to visiting taverns.[469]

After an hour of drinking, twenty-one-year-old Benjamin Fuder returned home and began partaking in pre-bar activities. A short time later, he went to a second story bedroom and returned with a large plastic bag of psychedelic mushrooms. Fuder offered to share the bag's contents, but the four others present smartly declined. After ingesting some of the mushrooms, Fuder again went upstairs and, a short time later, poked his head around the corner to ask "if anyone wanted to smoke a bowl" of marijuana. Once again, the other pregame participants politely declined.[470]

When Fuder returned downstairs, the alcohol continued to flow. As Schildt, Peterson, Vogel, and Crawford drank beer, Fuder downed a half-dozen shots of blackberry brandy and/or vodka. During a prior conversation, Fuder told Peterson he enjoyed going for walks in the Kettle Moraine State Forest a few miles east of Whitewater while "tripping on shrooms."[471]

At about 9:45 p.m., the pregame festivities ended and the five men walked to the Hawk's Nest at 214 W. Whitewater Avenue. Peterson bought a large "boot" of beer and shared about two beers from the plastic container with Fuder, who further consumed an additional shot and beer.[472]

An hour later, the men departed the Hawk's Nest and walked three blocks to the Mad Boar, where Fuder drank two or three more beers "and might have taken some shots." Fuder began getting "pretty hyped up" and began "playing basketball [absent a ball or rim] and dancing by himself." Witnessing his roommate's increasingly bizarre behavior, Schildt told Fuder he should "settle down a little bit."[473]

The barhopping continued and the five men walked to the College Pub. Once there, Fuder began speaking to a small group of women. The four other men openly complained that none of them particularly wanted to "babysit" their noticeably intoxicated colleague.[474]

With the College Pub filled to capacity, the five men agreed to leave and returned to the Hawk's Nest at 11:30 p.m. The owner of the bar, Matthew Golden, noticed Fuder "appeared very intoxicated." At 11:45 p.m., Schildt provided his roommate with a house key and told Fuder it was time to go home. Fuder left the tavern by himself.[475]

At around 12:30 a.m., Golden stepped outside the Hawk's Nest and observed Fuder standing in a parking lot between the bar and the Sweet Spot Coffee Shop. The intoxicated student started "wobbling" and "took off running" through a municipal parking lot. Fuder was wearing a navy blue Milwaukee Brewers t-shirt, khaki cargo pants, and tennis shoes. He also sported a distinguishable short, Mohawk haircut.[476]

Two hours later, the four party-goers returned to the S. Janesville Street residence. Schildt went straight to his bedroom and believed Fuder was asleep in his room. At 5:45 a.m., the four other men left for the golf course.[477]

An hour later, UW – Whitewater student, Ashley Maccaux, returned to her Whitewater residence after spending the night in the resort town of Lake Geneva. As she ascended the twenty steps to her second story apartment at 401 W. Center Street, Maccaux saw a wallet resting on the fifth step. The wallet was found to contain seventy-five dollars and Benjamin Fuder's Wisconsin driver's license. After sleeping for several hours, the conscientious twenty-two-year-old Maccaux turned the wallet over to Whitewater police officials.[478]

Sometime between 8:30 a.m. and 9 a.m., Brad Harris exited the front door of his home at 271 S. Church Street and saw a cellular telephone resting on the grass a foot from the sidewalk. Harris searched the telephone and dialed the number of the last person who had received a text message from the owner. A female, later identified as Fuder's girlfriend, Kelli Aide, asked Harris to place the phone in the mailbox at 403 S. Janesville Street.[479]

Similar to Hansel and Gretel's breadcrumbs, the recovery of Fuder's cellular telephone and wallet provided investigators with a path of travel. The wallet was located two-and-a-half blocks northwest of the Hawk's Nest, where Fuder was last seen running through a parking lot. The cellular phone in Harris' yard was a block west of the wallet recovery. Whitewater police, along with Fuder's friends and family, searched the downtown area for the missing student, but found no signs of the missing man.

After sunrise on July 29, a detective had a hunch and searched the area where Mark Wegener's body was found — the bottom of the Franklin Street quarry of Whitewater Limestone, Inc., about a half-mile south of the city limits. As he walked the lower area of the quarry, the detective spotted a blue object near the northeast inner wall. A closer look revealed a dead human body "in a face down position." The right leg suffered "an obvious femoral fracture due to an unnatural positioning." The dead man's hands where under the shoulders, which suggested he had sought to break the seventy foot fall into the darkness. The deceased also suffered "significant facial trauma." Post mortem lividity was observed on the dead man's head and lower extremities, an indication the body had not been moved. Although no identification was found on the deceased, the clothing, body type, and Mohawk haircut matched the description of Benjamin Fuder.[480]

After Fuder's body was recovered, officers responded to his residence and received written consent from his roommate, Michael Schildt, to search the home. In the dead man's bedroom, investigators located a gram scale, "55.6 grams of psilocin and 17.6 grams of THC, paraphernalia and two pills of clear capsules of an unknown orange powder."[481]

An autopsy determined Fuder died from head trauma from the fall into the quarry. A toxicology tests indicated his BAC was 0.11. Marijuana and psilocin (psychedelic mushrooms) were also found in his system.[482]

The relatively modest blood alcohol level was telling. At six-foot-five and two hundred-and-fifteen pounds, Fuder was a big man. Based on the statements of witnesses, however, his estimated BAC at 11:30 p.m. was somewhere in the neighborhood of 0.15. The 0.04 difference suggests several hours passed from the time Fuder left the Hawk's Nest to his fall at the quarry. Last seen running through a municipal parking lot at 12:30 a.m. and "tripping" on mushrooms, Fuder may have decided, as he had on prior occasions, to hike into the woods. Located adjacent to S. Franklin Street, the quarry of Whitewater Limestone, Inc. was just two miles south of the apartment steps where the deceased student's wallet was recovered.[483]

Although the Walworth County Coroner's Office listed the death as accidental, Fuder's brother, Joshua, told the UW – Whitewater student newspaper something was amiss. "My brother and Mark [Wegener] may very well have been drunk or under the influence of other substances at the time of their death, but to me, that is not a good enough explanation for what happened to these promising young men."[484]

We will never know how much promise Benjamin Fuder's life may have had. Like the "very bright" individuals in the United Kingdom's *National Child Development Study*, he choose to live on the edge by experimenting with mind-altering drugs. In the end, this risky behavior resulted in a life ending, psychedelic plunge.

Backroads Blunder

In his book, *Arrest-Proof Yourself*, Dale Carson, a former Miami-Dade police officer turned defense attorney, offers four "golden rules" to avoid spending a night in jail. One key provision is to figuratively become invisible to law enforcement. "If police can't see you," Carson explained, "they can't arrest you." If an individual is going to commit crime, the attorney suggests doing so at home, a place protected by the Fourth Amendment.[485]

Making one's self invisible from the police in a public place is more difficult. "Many people are aware that the 'take the back-road home' scheme is a common strategy for drunk drivers," a report in the *Bluefield Daily Telegraph* noted. "It's a sad but true reality." Lowering one's profile may be a clever way to avoid detection, but doing so can be a fool's errand. The death of Shalim Augustine in La Crosse, Wisconsin, is a prime example.[486]

On June 26, 2012, Augustine was arrested by a University of Wisconsin – La Crosse campus police officer for a second offense of operating a motor vehicle while intoxicated. The twenty-three-year-old restaurant employee quickly posted $500 bail and was released from the La Crosse County jail. One of the conditions of his release was to stay absolutely sober. Thirteen days later, he decided to ignore the order not to drink.[487]

On July 9, at about 5:15 p.m., Steve Chmura arrived at his friend's place of employment, Huck Finn's on the Water, a restaurant/tavern located on the west bank of the Black River. Upon greeting Augustine, Chmura could tell he had already been drinking. After downing two or three more drinks, the two men and two female acquaintances left for a boating excursion on the Mississippi River. While on the water, Augustine had two or three more beers. The four then went to the Pettibone Boat Club, a trendy summer boaters' hangout located on a Mississippi River peninsula. Here, Augustine slammed two or three more alcoholic beverages. Traveling over four miles upriver, the party docked at a houseboat on the Black River near Copeland Park. Over the course of the next hour, Augustine drank two or three VO whiskeys and became noticeably intoxicated.[488]

Around midnight, Chmura took the boat one hundred-and-fifty yards upriver and moored the craft to a pier just west of Logan Street. As the hungry party-goers walked to a nearby Kwik Trip convenience store, Augustine turned to Emily Dresen and said, "I gotta go," and staggered south from the rear of Powerhouse Marine towards the train in Copeland Park.[489]

Augustine resided four-and-a-half miles south of Copeland Park at 1809 Hyde Avenue. Although he had a cellular telephone in his possession, the intoxicated man had left a set of keys on the houseboat and his car parked at Huck Finn's on the Water. Dresen told investigators Augustine "did not want to get caught drinking." To avoid being arrested for bail jumping, he likely sought to remain invisible to the police by using sparsely traveled side streets to get home.[490]

Early into the probe of the man's disappearance, a common theme emerged: Augustine's reputation as a hard-partier. Huck Finn's manager, Patricia Baumgartner, told an investigator Augustine frequently became "fall down drunk." Present in the room at the time, other friends and co-workers concurred with Baumgartner's depiction of the missing man's drinking habits. The restaurant's manager reiterated that Augustine was "very worried" about violating the no-drink order and "would avoid walking along the main streets in La Crosse on his way home to stay away from the police." She believed the intoxicated man would "find a back way home," which is why Baumgartner advised search teams to check the marsh trails, Houska Park, Riverside Park, Black River Beach and Copeland Park.[491]

On July 10, with Augustine still in the wind, La Crosse police requested the assistance of Jackson County Sheriff Deputy Chief Mark Moen and his two canines. Moen was provided with two articles of the missing man's clothes as scent objects. Each dog separately tracked Augustine and both followed a scent path from the rear of Powerhouse Marine south to the Copeland Park tennis courts. The dogs did not follow a patch to the banks of the Black River.[492]

Aware that Augustine was in possession of his cellular telephone, investigators contacted Sprint and requested a ping, but the device was turned off. The best Sprint could do was provide an approximate address of the telephone's last known location — 5405 Keil Coulee Road, a rural area five-and-a-half-miles east of Powerhouse Marine.[493]

Cellular telephone records showed Taylor Yamamoto, an employee at the Pettibone Boat Club and a former co-worker of the missing man, was the last person to call Augustine on July 8 at 9:46 p.m. A friend of Augustine's, Casey Brown, sent a text message at 10:38 p.m., but an impaired Augustine never responded. For the next two-and-half hours, no calls or texts were made or sent. From 1:02 to 2:27 a.m., Steve Chmura, concerned he had yet to hear from Augustine, made thirty-nine unsuccessful attempts to contact his friend. The telephone records made it clear a ride was never requested or a cab summoned.[494]

On July 11 at about 6 p.m., Anthony Espe, his daughter, and her two friends, tubed along the Black River just south of the I-90 Bridge. Espe spotted what he believed was a log floating in the water. As he paddled closer, Espe observed the upper body and head of a human body above the water. He circled around the corpse and used his mobile telephone to contact the police.[495]

A La Crosse police river patrol boat responded to the area and located the body, which had oddly moved fifty yards north against the river's southern current. A short time later, the corpse was pulled aboard a La Crosse Fire Department rescue boat. In possession of the missing man's photograph, an investigator ascertained the dead man was Augustine.[496]

The only trauma on the body was some minor tissue tearing and swelling associated with a water saturation drowning and natural decomposition. A cellular telephone was located in the left front pants pocket of Augustine's cargo pants. A wallet containing money and his identification was inside the rear right pants pocket. Augustine's belt was "undone at the waist" and the fly of his pants half unbuttoned.[497]

The following day, the body was conveyed to the Dane County morgue for an autopsy. A forensic pathologist found "no external or internal signs of trauma or injury." A toxicology report listed Augustine's BAC at 0.323, four times over the legal limit to drive.[498]

Investigators surmised Augustine accidentally drowned while trying to relieve himself. Two matters, however, remained unresolved: The recovery of Augustine's body upriver from where the dogs hit on his scent, and the last known location of his cellular telephone five-and-a-half miles to the east of Copeland Park.

To determine the Black River's current, a La Crosse police investigator met with experts from the Wisconsin Department of Natural Resources (DNR) and the US Army Corps of Engineers. John Sullivan, a retired Mississippi River quality specialist, explained the surface currents of the Black River are influenced by wind. As such, surface winds from the south could push objects, such as logs, "north at a fast pace." A surge of high water from the Mississippi River could also cause the Black River's currents to "reverse for a distance." As a result, it was possible Augustine's body was carried a mile-and-a- half upriver to the I-90 Bridge.[499]

The last known location of Augustine's cellular telephone, at 5405 Keil Coulee Road, was inconclusive. Deputies from the La Crosse County Sheriff's Office went to the rural residence and were unable to make contact with the occupants of the home. Yet, as the Joseph Sjoberg investigation illustrated, last known cellular telephone locations generally encompass a broad radius. As such, investigators concluded Augustine did not travel far after leaving his friends near Powerhouse Marine.[500]

In all likelihood, Shalim Augustine's effort to remain invisible from the police took him to the banks of the Black River. Patricia Baumgartner, the manager of Huck Finn's on the Water, told police "Shalim is very scared of water and can't swim." If Augustine stumbled and fell into the Black River while relieving himself, the highly intoxicated man would have been swept away by the fast paced, upriver current.[501]

CONCLUSION

From 1997 – 2014, twenty-nine otherwise healthy young men died primarily, although not exclusively, due to their own negligence. Many of those who perished had promising futures. By the grace of God, one can only imagine how many of today's movers and shakers could have met similar fates. After all, most attended college and some engaged in risky behaviors. One thing is clear, though: I can confidently state none of these men died at the hands of a serial killer.

The elimination of a mass murderer as a suspect does not negate the possibility of foul play in at least three deaths. Although he was highly intoxicated, Richard Hlavaty, fearful of being beaten, was chased into the Mississippi River by a group of men. Once in the water, at least one man on shore threw large rocks in his direction. In Wisconsin, there is no statute of limitations for homicide; therefore, a possibility still exists someone could be charged with Hlavaty's death.

Another case with an ambiguous set of circumstances is the death of Russell Plummer, whose body was found in an isolated wooded area east of Bloomer, Wisconsin. Investigators did not recover any firearms from the deceased man's vehicle. I found it rather odd that a sober, rugged outdoorsmen would visit the woods with no intent to hunt. Did Plummer plan to rendezvous with someone? If so, his cellular telephone records offered few clues.

Sober people do sometimes die in the woods. A November 2005 incident is a prime example. The *U.S. Center for Disease Control* (CDC) reported a forty-nine-year-old man exited his car to hunt in a wooded area prior to sunset. While lost in the darkness, the man hiked nearly six miles across tough terrain. As the temperature dipped to twenty-eight degrees, a mixture of precipitation fell during the night. A search and rescue team located the missing man the following evening.[502]

"The man was found dressed in thermal underwear, jeans, wool socks, sneakers, a cotton shirt, an oil-cloth coat, and a cowboy hat," the CDC noted. "All of his clothing was wet, and he smelled of wood smoke. He was carrying his rifle and a global positioning system unit. Trackers determined the man had stumbled and fallen several times. When found, the man was unresponsive and cyanotic; his body was stiff, and he had no detectable respiration or pulse. After several hours of backcountry transport, the man was pronounced dead. The coroner certified death as fatal arrhythmia resulting from severe hypothermia."[503]

Similar to the deceased man in the CDC report, Plummer, whose cellular telephone was found inside his vehicle, took a tumble down a steep embankment and likely became disoriented. He appeared to be in the process of building a makeshift shelter, slipped on a tree branch, and fell for a second time. Still, the purpose of Plummer's presence in the woods and the reason for his initial fall have yet to be explained. After reading through the police reports and viewing the satellite imagery of the area, I have a gut feeling something, somewhere was missed.

The third case is the Green Bay drowning death of Jesse Archer. Based on the totality of the circumstances, this matter merits further investigation. Although detectives located video from a tavern Archer had patronized when he was alive, the police reports suggest they did not check the casino's surveillance footage. The man who had accompanied Archer to the casino was allegedly involved in a drug distribution scheme and Archer was allegedly in possession of a large quantity of pills, which were never recovered. Several weeks after the missing man's body was found in the Fox River, the man who had accompanied Archer to the casino told investigators he simply left and walked home. As it relates to the date of Archer's disappearance, police reports show investigators did not obtain the man's address and failed to corroborate his statement. A short time after speaking with this man via telephone, investigators seemingly took the convicted felon's statement at face value and closed the case.

Three of the remaining twenty-six deaths involved suicides. Under mental duress on the anniversary of a friend's suicide, Gordon Stumblin, a man with a history of schizophrenia and substance abuse, disappeared after making a bizarre telephone call. His body was later found in the Mississippi River near La Crosse.

Solid detective work resulted in the clearances of two cases that emanated from Madison, Wisconsin. Twenty-year-old Japanese exchange student Kenji Ohmi's journal entries told of a troubled young man who sought to end his life. On a cold January morning, video footage captured him leaving his apartment. Ohmi apparently walked onto Lake Mendota until the thin ice gave way.

Another Madison man, Joseph Sjoberg, drove to a wooden area outside of Columbus, Wisconsin. While inside his car, the troubled young man set his vehicle ablaze with gasoline. Investigators learned Sjoberg had conducted Internet searches on ways to make a car explode.

Of the twenty-three remaining cases, the one that caught my attention was the September 1997 drowning death of Charles Blatz, the first accidental strange drowning death in a series of ten investigated by the La Crosse Police Department. Although foul play was not involved, a significant gap of time — from 12:30 a.m. when Blatz left Sneaker's bar until 2:30 a.m. bar time — existed. In 1997, the proliferation of affordable and reliable surveillance systems had yet to occur, which likely explains how the highly intoxicated UW — Platteville student, in town for La Crosse's annual Oktoberfest celebration, seemingly walked away without notice.

Unlike many of the other inebriated students who lost their lives, Blatz was a mature military veteran turned engineering major. U.S. military personnel are stationed around the globe and sometimes patronize seedy entertainment districts. To ensure their safety, soldiers, airmen, and sailors often travel in groups. Therefore, I found it unusual a military veteran would simply wander off alone. Then again, an over indulgence of alcohol can equate to a lapse of good judgment.

In an effort to clear up some loose ends concerning several of these investigations, I sent letters to a number of relatives, but most, including two to the Blatz family, went unanswered. Whether it was the fees charged by charlatan psychics, the use of a sketchy canine search company or the former detectives' advocacy of the smiley face killer theory, family members, it seemed, had had enough. After all, the emotional trauma that comes with losing a child or a sibling to an unnatural death is akin to a significant wound, which, even after it heels, often leaves a noticeable scar.

REFERENCES

(Endnotes)

1   Ronald K. Wright, Eds Stuart H. James and John J. Norby *Forensic Science: An Introduction to Scientific and Investigative Techniques*. 3ʳᵈ Ed. (CRC Press, Francis & Taylor Group, Boca Raton, FL, 2009), 55.

2   Gary Haupt, "Drowning Investigations," *FBI Law Enforcement Bulletin*, Vol. 75, No. 2, February 2006, 14-21.

3   Ibid., 15-20.

4   Titan TV, "Oshkosh Cold Case," youtube.com, January 5, 2016, https://www.youtube.com/watch?v=x7DVTodIeHE, accessed September 28, 2016.

5   Ibid.

6   Ibid.; *Oshkosh Northwestern*, October 15, 1965, p. 21; Helen Young, Milwaukee County Assistant Medical Examiner, Official Autopsy Protocol Report, October 17, 1965; Appleton Post-Crescent, December 8, 1965, p. B1.

7   Titan TV, "Oshkosh Cold Case," youtube.com, January 5, 2016, https://www.youtube.com/watch?v=x7DVTodIeHE, accessed September 28, 2016.

8   Ibid., Helen Young, Milwaukee County Assistant Medical Examiner, Official Autopsy Protocol Report, October 17, 1965.

9   *Appleton Post-Crescent*, December 8, 1965, p. B1; *Kenosha News*, December, 11, 1965, p. 2.

10   *Neenah-Menasha Northwestern*, December 9, 1965, p. 1.

11   *Neenah-Menasha Northwestern*, October 20, 1965, p. 1.

12   Daniel Buhr interviewed, November 4, 2016.

13   *Appleton Post-Crescent*, October 24, 1965, p. B1.

14   Titan TV, "Oshkosh Cold Case," *youtube.com*, January 5, 2016, https://www.youtube.com/watch?v=x7DVTodIeHE, accessed September 28, 2016.

15   *The Quiver*, the official year book of the Wisconsin State University at Oshkosh, "Football – 1965" team photograph, 269; Roster of "W.S.U. Oshkosh" football team, 1965, provided by Keenan Timm, University of Wisconsin – Oshkosh athletic archivist.

16   Arthur Marwick, The Sixties Cultural Revolution in Britain, France, Italy, and the United States, c.1958-c.1974 (London: Bloomsbury Reader, 2012), 3; "The Homosexual in America," Metafilter.com, January 21, 1966 exert from *Time*, http://www.metafilter.com/93018/Time-magazine-on-homosexuality-the-50s-through-the-70s, accessed October 20, 2016.

17   John D'Emilio, The World Turned: Essays on Gay History, Politics, and Culture (Durham, NC: Duke University Press, 2002), 200.

18   Harriet Ryan, "Police Officer Convicted of Killing Gay Lover," *cnn.com*, May 23, 2005, http://www.cnn.com/2005/LAW/05/23/rios/ (accessed October 20, 2016).

19   Ibid.

20   Investigator J. Korger, La Crosse Police Department, official police report, Case #97-30991, July 12, 1997, p. 2; Detective J. Dunham, La Crosse Police Department, official police report, Case #97-303991, July 16, 1997, p. 2.

21   Ibid, pp. 2 & 4.

22   Ibid., p. 2.

23   Detective J. Dunham, La Crosse Police Department, official police report, Case #97-303991, July 16, 1997, p. 2.

24   Ibid., p. 3; Officer Ronald Secord, La Crosse Police Department, official police report, Case #97-303991, July 12, 1997, p. 2.

25   Officer Rick Pfenning, La Crosse Police Department, official police report, Case #97-303991, July 12, 1997, p. 1.

26   Detective J. Dunham, La Crosse Police Department, official police report, Case #97-30991, July 16, 1997, p. 3.

27   Investigator J. Korger, La Crosse Police Department, official police report, Case #97-303991, July 14, 1997, p. 3.

28   Ibid.

29   Ibid.

30   Ibid., pp. 3 & 4; Footprints from the Edge, "Richard Hlavaty" July 11, 1997, http://footprintsattheriversedge.blogspot.com/2006/11/richard-hlavaty-19-lacrosse-wi-july.html (accessed October 25, 2016).

31   C. Joholski, La Crosse Police Department, official police report, Case #97-30991, July 14, 1997, p. 2.

32   Detective J. Dunham, La Crosse Police Department, official police report, Case #97-30991, July 16, 1997, p. 4.

33   Ibid.

34   Ibid., p. 5.

35   Ibid.

36   Ibid., p. 6.

37   Ibid.

38   Detective Ryan Fitzgerald, La Crosse Police Department, official police report, Case #97-30991, April 7, 2014, p. 1.

39   Ibid., p. 4.

40   Ibid.

41   Ibid., p. 6.

42   Ibid.

43   Lieutenant M. Brohmer, La Crosse Police Department, official police report, Case #97-45167, October 3, 1997, p. 1.

44   Ibid., p. 2.

45   Investigator G. Leque, La Crosse Police Department, official police report, Case #97-46167, September 30, 1997, p. 1.

46   Lieutenant M. Brohmer, La Crosse Police Department, official police report, Case #97-45167, October 3, 1997, p. 2.

47   Officer Holanka, La Crosse Police Department, official police report, Case #97-46167, October 3, 1997, p. 1.

48   Officer Jack Johnson, La Crosse Police Department, official police report, Case #97-46167, October 5, 1997, pp. 1 & 2.

49   Lieuteant M. Brohmer, La Crosse Police Department, official police report, Case #97-45167, October 3, 1997, p. 3.

50   Ibid., p. 4.

51   Ibid.

52   Ibid.

53   Lieutenant M. Brohmer, La Crosse Police Department, official police report, Case #97-45167, October 3, 1997, p. 2.

54   Chiung M. Chen, Mary C. Dufour and Hsiao-ye Y, "Alcohol Consumption Among Young Adults Ages 18–24 in the United States: Results From the 2001–2002 NESARC Survey," *National Institute on Alcohol Abuse and Alcoholism*, http://pubs.niaaa.nih.gov/publications/arh284/269-280.htm (accessed October 27, 2016).

55   Rachel Durfee, "The World's Hardest-Partying Generation? Cyber-Millennials," *popsi.com*, May 13, 2009, http://www.popsci.com/environment/article/2009-05/cyber-millenials-are-drinking-more-you-and-theyre-older (accessed October 28, 2016).

56   Sergeant J. Korger, La Crosse Police Department, official police report, Case #97-46167, September 18, 1999, p. 1.

57   Ibid.

58   Allan Low, transcribed statement to La Crosse police, Case #97-46902, October 9, 1997.

59   Investigator D.J. Marcou, La Crosse Police Department, official police report, Case #97-46902, October 8, 1997, p. 2; Ryan Torgerson, transcribed statement to La Crosse police, Case #97-46902, October 10, 1997, p. 2.

60   Investigator D.J. Marcou, La Crosse Police Department, official police report, Case #97-46902, October 8, 1997, p. 1.

61   Ibid., *St. Paul Pioneer Press*, October 12, 1997, 5B.,

62   Ibid.; *Green Bay Press-Gazette*, October 22, 1997, p. 9; Footprints from the Edge, "Anthony Skifton, 19, La Crosse, WI," October 5, 1997, http://footprintsattheriversedge.blogspot.com/2006/11/100597-anthony-skifton-19-la-crosse-wi.html (accessed October 30, 2016).

63   Investigator B. Burke, La Crosse Police Department, official police report, Case #97-46902, October 13, 1997, p. 3.

64   Ibid.

65   Ibid.

66   Dan Springer, "Officials: Alcohol was Killer," *The Chippewa Herald*, April 24, 2004, http://chippewa.com/news/officials-alcohol-was-killer/article_f599dbf9-0d6a-5ebb-ba4d-79bc25863922.html (accessed October 30, 2016).

67   Larry Oakes, Oktoberfest in La Crosse: A Party Town Tries to Sober Up," *StarTribune.com*, October 3, 2012, http://www.startribune.com/oktoberfest-in-la-crosse-a-party-town-tries-to-sober-up/171948771/ (accessed October 31, 2016).

68   Lieutenant M. Brohmer, La Crosse Police Department, official police report, Case #98-8847, interview of Angie Truttman, March 4, 1998, p. 2.

69   Lieutenant M. Brohmer, La Crosse Police Department, official police report, Case #98-8847, interview of Kevin McDermott, March 3, 1998, p. 1.

70   Lieutenant M. Brohmer, La Crosse Police Department, official police report, Case #98-8847, interview of Ryan Goodno, March 20, 1998, pp. 1 & 2.

71   Christopher Kaufmann, written statement to La Crosse Police Department, Case #98-8847, March 2, 1998.

72   Officer Secord, La Crosse Police Department, official police report, Case #98-8847, February 22, 1998, pp. 1 & 2.

73   Lieutenant M. Brohmer, La Crosse Police Deparment, official police report, "exceptional clearance," June 17, 1998, pp. 1 & 2.

74   Officer Coady, La Crosse Police Department, official police report, Case #98-8847, February 23, 1998.

75   Lieutenant M. Brohmer, La Crosse Police Department, official police report, "exceptional clearance," June 17, 1998, p 3.

76   Ibid.

77   Ibid.

78   Ibid.; Detective D. Schatzley, La Crosse Police Department, official police report, Case #98-8847, April 4, 1998, p. 2.

79   Lieutenant M. Brohmer, La Crosse Police Department, official police report, "exceptional clearance," June 17, 1998, p 5.

80   Wisconsin State Statute 343.303; National Highway Safety Training Administration, "Special Testing for Possible Alcohol Carrying Over Effects Using the Intoximeters, Inc., Alco-Sensor IV at 10 C," March 2002, http://www.nhtsa.gov/people/injury/research/carryout/ (accessed November 2, 2016).

81   American Prosecutors Research institute, "Admissibility of Horizontal Gaze Nystagmus Evidence," *ndaa.org*, 2003, http://www.ndaa.org/pdf/admissibility%20of%20hgn_april_2003.pdf (accessed November 2, 2016).

82   Lieuteant M. Brohmer, La Crosse Police Department, official police report, Case #98-8847, December 14, 1999, p. 2.

83   Ibid.

84   Ibid., p. 3.

85   Lieutenant M. Brohmer, La Crosse Police Department, official police report, interview of Angie Truttman, Case #98-8847, March 4, 1998, p. 1.

86   *Wisconsin v. Jeffrey F. Geesey*, Portage County Case #1998CT000189, Wisconsin Circuit Court Access, August 31, 1998, https://wcca.wicourts.gov/courtRecordEvents.do;jsessionid=2835D4BAE18036005472DA61C310EA56.render6?caseNo=1998CT000189&countyNo=49&cacheId=6987BE449AC99D57ECE16789571E78E1&recordCount=2&offset=0&linkOnlyToForm=false&sortDirection=DESC (accessed November 4, 2016); Lieutenant Brohmer, La Crosse Police Department, official police report, Case #99-17838, August 30, 1999, p. 2.

87   Officer Mark Rosenmeier, La Crosse Police Department, official police report, Case #99-17838, April 15, 1999.

88   Ibid.; Lieutenant M. Brohmer, La Crosse Police Department, official police report, Case #99-17838, August 30, 1999, p. 3.

89   Ibid., pp. 3 & 4.

90   Lieutenant M. Brohmer, La Crosse Police Department, official police report, Case #99-17838, interview of Seth Zondag, April 23, 1999, pp. 1 & 2; Lieutenant M. Brohmer, La Crosse Police Department, official police report, Case #99-17838, interview of Sean Glavich, April 23, 1999; Lieutenant M. Brohmer, La Crosse Police Department, official police report, Case #99-17838, interview of Sean Hager, p. 1.

91   Lieutenant M. Brohmer, La Crosse Police Department, official police report, Case #99-17838, interview of Dawn Van Geertruy, May 6, 1999, p.1.

92   Lieutenant M. Brohmer, La Crosse Police Department, official police report, Case #99-17838, interview of Nichole Loken, May 6, 1999, p. 2.

93   Lieutenant M. Brohmer, La Crosse Police Department, official police report, Case #99-17838, exceptional clearance, August 30, 1999, p. 5.

94   Ibid., 4; Lieutenant M. Brohmer, La Crosse Police Department, official police report, Case #99-17838, May 21, 1999; Lieutenant M. Brohmer, La Crosse Police Department, official

134

95   Lieutenant M. Brohmer, La Crosse Police Department, official police report, Case #99-17838, exceptional clearance, August 30, 1999, p. 6.

96   Ibid.

97   Ibid.; Footprints at the River's Edge, "Jeffrey Geesey, 21, La Crosse, WI," April 13, 1999, http://footprintsattheriversedge.blogspot.com/2006/11/041399-jeffrey-geesey-la-crosse-wi.html (accessed November 4, 2016).

98   Officer Korn, La Crosse Police Department, official police report, Case #99-17838, May 24, 1999.

99   Lieutenant M. Brohmer, La Crosse Police Department, official police report, Case #99-17838, exceptional clearance, August 30, 1999, p. 7; *Wisconsin State Journal*, May 13, 2004, p. B5.

100   Lieutenant M. Brohmer, La Crosse Police Department, official police report, Case #01-11465, exceptional clearance, March 2, 2001, p. 1.

101   Ibid., p. 2.

102   Ibid.

103   Ibid.

104   Ibid., p. 3.

105   Ibid., 4.

106   Officer J. Rush, Eau Claire Police Department, official police report, Case #02-24897, October 2, 2002.

107   Officer J. Trapp, Eau Claire Police Department, official police report, Case #02-24897, October r, 2002; Officer Ruppert, Eau Claire Police Department, official police report, Case #02-24897, October 4, 2002, pp. 1 & 2.

108   Officer McIntyre, Eau Claire Police Department, official police report, Case #02-24897, September 30, 2002, p. 2.

109   Officer Trapp, Eau Claire Police Department, official police report, Case #02-24897, October 5, 2002.

110   Officer Tollefson, Eau Claire Police Department, official police report, Case #02-24897, October 6, 2002.

111   Lieutenant Venaa, Eau Claire Police Department, official police report, Case #02-24897, October 6, 2002, pp. 1 & 2.

112   Officer Zwiefelhofer, Eau Claire Police Department, official police report, Case #02-24897, October 6, 2002, p. 1.

113   Ibid., 2.

114   Dr. Thomas W. Hadley, Autopsy report, Accession Case # A02-129, Sacred Heart Hospital, October 7, 2002, p. 2.

115   *St. Paul Pioneer Press*, November 12, 2002, p. 2B; *St. Paul Pioneer Press*, May 17, 2004, p. A1.

116   *St. Paul Pioneer Press*, November 5, 2005, p. 1B.

117   Officer Mikunda, Eau Claire Police Department, official police report, Case #02-28344, November 7, 2002, p. 3.

118   Officer Ruppert, Eau Claire Police Department, official police report, Case #02-28344, November 9, 2002, pp. 2 & 3.

119   *The Record* (St. John's University student newspaper), November 14, 2002, p. 1.

120   Ibid.

121   *The Record*, November 21, 2004, p. 1.

122   Officer Birtzer, Eau Claire Police Department, official police report, Case #02-28344, November 13, 2001, p. 1.

123   Ibid., p. 3.

124   Officer Walton, Eau Claire Police Department, official police report, Case #02-28344, November 11, 2002, p. 1.

125   Ibid.

126   Ibid.

127   Eau Claire Police News Release, November 11, 2002, Case #02-28344.

128   Officer Mikunda, Eau Claire Police Department, official police report, Case #02-28344, November 7, 2002, p. 1.

129   Detective Paul Becker, Affidavit is Support of Subpoena Application, Circuit Court of Eau Claire County, November 11, 2002; Detective Becker, Eau Claire Police Department, official police report, Case #02-28344, December 5, 2002, pp. 1 & 2.

130   *Wisconsin State Journal*, November 19, 2002, p. B3.

131   Anonymous email, to Eau Claire Public Safety, regarding missing person, November 16, 2002.

132   George Reykdal, letter to the Eau Claire Police Department, received November 14, 2002.

133   Ibid.

134   Dallas S. Drake, Cheryl M. Bebernes, Brandon J. Wheeler, Eden Z. Stelflug, Peter D. Espenson, Angela M. Van Auken, Kevin R. Olson, Agathe M. Panaretos, & Ben J. Anderson, "Drowning the Smiley Face Murder Theory," *Center for Homicide Research*, 2010 (held by author).

135 Detective John Birtzer, Eau Claire Police Department, official police report, Case #02-28344, December 4, 2002, p. 1.

136 Ibid., pp. 1 & 2.

137 Officer Johnson, Eau Claire Police Department, official police report, Case #02-28344, November 24, 2001, p. 1.

138 Ibid., p. 2.

139 Ibid.

140 Ibid.; Eau Claire Police Department, "Wanted by the Eau Claire Police Department: Amort, Thomas James," November 2002.

141 Detective John Birtzer, Eau Claire Police Department, official police report, Case #02-28344, December 4, 2002, p. 2.

142 Deputy Chief of Police Gary Foster, Eau Claire Police Department, memo to Patrol C.O.'s, regarding "Noll Search Status," November 26, 2002.

143 Deputy Chief of Police Gary Foster, Eau Claire Police Department, official police report, Case #02-28344, December 5, 2002, p. 1.

144 Ibid., p. 2.

145 Detective John Birtzer, Eau Claire Police Department, official police report, Case #02-28344, December 6, 2002, p. 1.

146 Ibid., 2.

147 Janet L. Fitzgerald, letter to the Eau Claire Police Department, December 21, 2002.

148 Officer Mark Pieper, Eau Claire Police Department, official police report, Case #03-006352, March 25, 2003, p. 1.

149 Detective John Birtzer, Eau Claire Police Department, official police report, Case #02-28344, , March 25, 2003, p. 1.

150 Ibid., p. 2.

151 Eau Claire Parks Department, "Half Moon Lake," http://www.ci.eau-claire.wi.us/departments/recreation-services/parks/boat-landings-fishing/half-moon-lake (accessed November 20, 2016); Gary Haupt, "Drowning Investigations," FBI Law Enforcement Bulletin, February, 2006, p. 16 (held by author); Weather Underground, "Weather History for Eau Claire, Wisconsin," November 6, 2002, https://www.wunderground.com/history/airport/KEAU/2002/11/6/DailyHistory.html?req_city=&req_state=&req_statename=&reqdb.zip=&reqdb.magic=&reqdb.wmo= (accessed November 16, 2016).

152 Gary Haupt, "Drowning Investigations," FBI Law Enforcement Bulletin, February, 2006, p. 16 (held by author).

153 Ibid., 15; Saint Paul Globe, July 18, 1887, p. 1.

154 Green Bay Press-Gazette, December 29, 2002, p. 18.

155   Ibid.

156   Ibid.

157   *Green Bay Press-Gazette*, March 16, 2003, p. 12.

158   Collection Services, "01/10/03: Nathan Herr, 21, Sheboygan, WI," http://www.collectionservice.info/article/511361952/01-10-03-nathan-herr-21-sheboygan-wi/ (accessed November 27, 2016).

159   Footprints at the River's Edge, "12/12/02: Chad Sharon, 18, South Bend, IN," http://footprintsattheriversedge.blogspot.com/2006/11/121202-chad-sharon-south-bend-in.html (accessed November 27, 2016).

160   Ibid.; *The Republic* (Columbus, IN), February 27, 2003, p. 5.

161   Ibid.

162   Gary Haupt, "Drowning Investigations," *FBI Law Enforcement Bulletin*, February 2006, 20; Footprints at the River's Edge, "Chris Jenkins Homicide: Someone Knows Something," November 1, 2013, http://footprintsattheriversedge.blogspot.com/2013/11/chris-jenkins-homicide-someone-knows.html (accessed November 28, 2016); Kevin Gannon and D. Lee Gibertson, Case Study in Drowning Forensics (Baton Raton, FL: CRC Press, 2014), 140-141

163   Ibid.; *Racine Journal Times*, May 13, 2003, p. 5.

164   Gannon and Gibertson, *Case Study in Drowning Forensics*, 119 – 120.

165   Ibid., 141.

166   U.S. Center for Disease Control, "Gamma Hydroxy Butyrate Use -- New York and Texas, 1995-1996," April 4, 1997, http://www.cdc.gov/mmwr/preview/mmwrhtml/00047106.htm (accessed November 29, 2016); Drugs.com, "GHB or Gamma-Hydroxybutyrate," https://www.drugs.com/illicit/ghb.html (accessed November 28, 2016).

167   *Green Bay Press-Gazette*, March 16, 2003, p. 12; Footprints at the River's Edge, "01/10/03: Nathan Herr, 21, Sheboygan, WI," http://footprintsattheriversedge.blogspot.com/2006/11/011003-nathan-herr-sheboygan-wi.html (accessed November 27, 2016).

168   Ibid.

169   U.S. Center for Disease Control, "10 Leading Causes of Injury Deaths by Age Group Highlighting Violence -

Related Injury Deaths, United States," 2009, https://www.cdc.gov/injury/wisqars/pdf/leading_causes_injury_deaths_age_group_highlighting_violence-related-injury_deaths_us_2009-a.pdf (accessed December 1, 2016); Dallas S. Drake, Cheryl M. Bebernes, Brandon J.

Wheeler, Eden Z. Stelflug, Peter D. Espenson, Angela M. Van Auken, Kevin R. Olson, Agathe M. Panaretos, & Ben J. Anderson, "Drowning the Smiley Face Murder Theory," *Center for Homicide Research,* 2010, http://homicidecenter.org/wp-content/uploads/2012/03/Research-Brief-on-Smiley-Face-Murder-Theory-FINAL.pdf (accessed December 1, 2016);

170   Rhonda Stokes, "Drowning Prevention," *Maryland Department of Health and Mental*

138

Hygiene

Division of Community Service, Spring 2007, http://phpa.dhmh.maryland.gov/OEHFP/CHS/
Shared%20Documents/drwnngprevtn%20ycoptrs.pdf (accessed December 1, 2016).

171   Ibid.

172   Footprints at the River's Edge, "12/05/03: Gordon Stumlin, 37, La Crosse, WI," http://
footprintsattheriversedge.blogspot.com/2008/04/120503-gordon-stumlin-37-la-crosse-wi.html
(accessed December 1, 2016).

173   La Crosse Police Department, official police report, Case #03-57651, December 9, 2003,
p. 1.

174   Lieutenant B. Burke, La Crosse Police Department, official police report, Case #04-17179,
June 8, 2004, p. 4.

175   Ibid., p. 2 & 3; Officer Eric Christenson, La Crosse Police Department, official police
report, Case #04-17179, April 10, 2004, p. 7.

176   La Crosse Police, official police report, Case #04-17179, interview of Kristine Schultz,
April 13, 2004.

177   Lieutenant B. Burke, La Crosse Police Department, official police report, Case #04-17179,
June 8, 2004, p. 7.

178   Officer James Kirby, La Crosse Police Department, official police report, Case #04-
171709 (related Case #03-45155), January 1, 2005.

179   Lieutenant B. Burke, La Crosse Police Department, official police report, Case #04-17179,
June 8, 2004, p. 8.

180   Ibid., p. 9.

181   Ibid.; Officer E. Christenson, La Crosse Police Department, official police report, Case
#04-17179, April 10, 2004, p. 3.

182   *Green Bay Press-Gazette*, April 29, 2004, p. 8.

183   Ibid.

184   Matt Erickson, Myears Apologizes to Family," *Brainerd Dispatch*, June 29, 2006, http://
www.brainerddispatch.com/content/myears-apologizes-family (accessed December 3, 2016);
Associated Press, "Dahlquist's Body Found After 18-Month Search," *USA Today*, May 16, 2004,
http://usatoday30.usatoday.com/news/nation/2004-05-16-body-minnesota_x.htm (accessed
December 3, 2016).

185   *Santa Cruz Sentinel*, May 16, 2004, p. 6.

186   Ibid.

187   Ibid.

188   Ibid.; Detective R. Burke, La Crosse Police Department, official police report, Case #04-
17179, November 26, 2004, p. 1.

189   *Santa Cruz Sentinel*, May 16, 2004, p. 6.

190   Detective M. Blokhuis, La Crosse Police Department, official police report, Case #04-26822, June 5, 2004.

191   Ibid.

192   S. Holinka, La Crosse Police Department, official police report, Case #04-26822, June 5, 2004, pp. 1 & 2.

193   Footprints at the River's Edge, "12/05/03: Gordon Stumlin, 37, La Crosse, WI," http://footprintsattheriversedge.blogspot.com/2008/04/120503-gordon-stumlin-37-la-crosse-wi.html (accessed December 1, 2016).

194   UW-Eau Claire Spectator, "Autopsy Reveals Alcohol in Body," December 6, 2004, *uwspectatornews.com*, http://www.spectatornews.com/campus-news/2004/12/06/autopsy-reveals-alcohol-in-body/ (retrieved December 7, 2016); UW-Eau Claire Spectator, "Friends Remember Miller's Good Mood," *spectatornews.com*, September 16, 2004, http://www.spectatornews.com/campus-news/2004/09/16/friends-remember-millers-good-mood/ (accessed December 7, 2016); Footprints at the River's Edge, "09/12/04: Jesse Miller, 21, Eau Claire, WI," http://footprintsattheriversedge.blogspot.com/2004/09/091204-jesse-miller-21-eau-claire-wi.html (accessed December 7, 2016).

195   UW-Eau Claire Spectator, "Autopsy Reveals Alcohol in Body," December 6, 2004, *uwspectatornews.com*, http://www.spectatornews.com/campus-news/2004/12/06/autopsy-reveals-alcohol-in-body/ (retrieved December 7, 2016).

196   UW-Eau Claire Spectator, "Friends Remember Miller's Good Mood," *spectatornews.com*, September 16, 2004, http://www.spectatornews.com/campus-news/2004/09/16/friends-remember-millers-good-mood/ (accessed December 7, 2016).

197   UW-Eau Claire Spectator, "Autopsy Reveals Alcohol in Body," December 6, 2004, *uwspectatornews.com*, http://www.spectatornews.com/campus-news/2004/12/06/autopsy-reveals-alcohol-in-body/ (retrieved December 7, 2016).

198   Ibid.

199   Detective Eliopoulos, Eau Claire Police Department, official police report, Case #05-12916, June 12, 2005, p. 1.

200   Ibid., pp. 6 & 7.

201   Ibid.

202   Ibid.

203   Ibid.

204   Ibid.

205   Ibid.

206   Ibid., p. 13.

207   Ibid., p. 21.

140

208 Ibid.

209 Ibid.

210 Officer John Birtzer, Eau Claire Police Department, official police report, Case #05-12916, June 14, 2005, p. 24.

211 Ibid., Detective Eliopoulos, Eau Claire Police Department, official police report, Case #05-12916, June 12, 2005, p. 22; Ibid., p. 37 & 39.

212 Ibid., pp. 48 & 49.

213 Ibid., p. 51.

214 Ibid., p. 56; Wisconsin State Laboratory of Hygiene, Specimen #05FX011848, July 27, 2005.

215 Eugene Kane, "The Killer Nobody Wants to Talk About," *OnMilwaukee.com*, April 3, 2013, http://onmilwaukee.com/buzz/articles/smileyfacekiler.html (accessed December 9, 2016).

216 Ibid.; *Wisconsin State Journal*, May 13, 2004, p. B5.

217 Mark Ilgen and Felicia Kleinberg, "The Link between Substance Abuse, Violence, and Suicide," *Psychiatric Times*, January 20, 2011, http://www.psychiatrictimes.com/substance-use-disorder/link-between-substance-abuse-violence-and-suicide (accessed December 9, 2016).

218 Officer Scott McConnell, Madison Police Department, official police report, Case #06-10826, January 30, 2006, p. 1.

219 Ibid., p. 2.

220 Ibid.

221 Ibid., p. 1; Detective Gregory Esser, Madison Police Department, official police report, Case #06-10826, January 30, 2006, p. 2.

222 Officer Scott McConnell, Madison Police Department, official police report, Case #06-10826, January 30, 2006, p. 1; Detective Gregory Esser, Madison Police Department, official police report, Case #06-10826, January 30, 2006, p. 2.

223 Detective Marion Morgan, Madison Police Department, official police report, Case #06-10826, January 30, 2006, p. 1; Detective Gregory Esser, Madison Police Department, official police report, Case #06-10826, January 30, 2006, p. 1.

224 Officer Scott McConnell, Madison Police Department, official police report, Case #06-10826, January 30, 2006, p. 2; Detective Gregory Esser, Madison Police Department, official police report, interview of Ariel Eduardo Perez, Case #06-10826, January 30, 2006, p. 2.

225 Sergeant David McCaw, Madison Police Department, official police report, Case #06-10826, February 1, 2006.

226 Detective Gregg Luedtke, Madison Police Department, official police report, Case #06-10826, February 6, 2006, pp. 1 & 2.

227 Ibid, p. 2.

228 Detective Marion Morgan, Madison Police Department, official police report, interview of Shuji Kosumoto, Case #06-10826, January 31, 2006, p. 1.

229 Detective Gregory Esser, Madison Police Department, official police report, interview of Mary Jane Lunde, Case #06-10826, February 16, 2006; Detective Gregory Esser, Madison Police Department, official police report, interview of David Callender, Case #06-10826, February 20, 2006.

230 Detective Gregory Esser, Madison Police Department, official police report, interview of Glen Braud, Case #06-10826, February 17, 2006; Detective Gregory Esser, Madison Police Department, official police report, interview of Kathy Sandefur, Case #06-10826, March 1, 2006.

231 Detective Gregory Esser, Madison Police Department, official police report, contact with UW-Milwaukee Police Detective Paul Sorrell, Case #06-10826, March 2, 2006.

232 Detective Gregory Esser, Madison Police Department, official police report, interview of Patrick Cain, Case #06-10826, March 31, 2006.

233 Officer Matthew Kenny, Madison Police Department, official police report, Case #06-10826, April 25, 2006.

234 Detective David Miller, Madison Police Department, official police report, Case #06-10826, June 28, 2006.

235 Officer Linda Covert, Madison Police Department, official police report, Case #06-10826, June 19, 2006.

236 Detective Marion Morgan, Madison Police Department, official police report, Case #06-10826, June 20, 2006, p. 1; Detective Marion Morgan, Madison Police Department, official police report, Case #06-10826, July 24, 2006.

237 Lt. Gerald Staniszewski, Eau Claire Police Department, memo to Deputy Chief Venaas, April 28, 2006, p. 1.

238 Ibid., p. 2.

239 Ibid., p. 3.

240 *Democrat Chronicle* (Rochester, NY), May 5, 1997, p. 5.

241 *New York Times*, April 8, 1997, p. B1; *New York Times*, April 17, 1997, p. B3.

242 All Things Crime, "The Smiley Face Killer Theory Refuses to Die," All Things Crime Blog, http://www.allthingscrimeblog.com/2015/02/09/the-smiley-face-killer-theory-refuses-to-die/ (accessed December 16, 2016)

243 Ibid.

244 Anne Jungen, "Jerry and Patti Homan Talk about their Son's River Death and how they've Lived through the Past Year," *La Crosse Tribune*, October 2, 2007, http://lacrossetribune.com/news/jerry-and-patti-homan-talk-about-their-son-s-river/article_b13b03ac-75c5-52bb-82ff-f97f301daf32.html (accessed December 20, 2016); Detective M. Blokhuis, La Crosse Police

Department, official police report, interview of Maggie Woerpel, Case #06-47087, October 4, 2006, pp. 13-14.

245 Investigator M. Byerson, La Crosse Police Department, official police report, Case #06-47087, September 30, 2006, p. 1.

246 Officer Ray Serres, La Crosse Police Department, official police report, Case #06-47087, September 30, 2006.

247 Investigator J. Mancuso, La Crosse Police Department, official police report, Case #06-47087, September 30, 2006, p. 2.

248 Ibid.

249 Ibid.

250 Officer S. Kudron, La Crosse Police Department, official police report, Case #06-47087, September 30, 2006; Lt. Mix, La Crosse Police Department, official police report, Case #06-47087, September 30, 2006.

251 Investigator M. Byerson, La Crosse Police Department, official police report, Case #06-47087, October 5, 2006, p. 1.

252 Ibid., p. 2; John E. Reid & Associates, Inc., "The Reid Technique of Interview and Interrogation," http://mymassp.com/files/Telling%20the%20Truth.pdf (accessed December 21, 2016).

253 Investigator M. Byerson, La Crosse Police Department, official police report, Case #06-47087, October 5, 2006, p. 2.

254 Detective M Blokhuis, La Crosse Police Department, official police report, Case #06-47087, October 4, 2006, pp. 11-12.

255 Deputy Chris Fabry, La Crosse County Sheriff's Office, official police report, Case #06-47087, September 29, 2006.

256 Investigator M. Byerson, La Crosse Police Department, official police report, Case #06-47087, October 5, 2006, p. 3.

257 Ibid.

258 Ibid.

259 Ibid., pp. 3-4.

260 Ibid., p. 2; Detective M Blokhuis, La Crosse Police Department, official police report, Case #06-47087, October 4, 2006, pp. 11-12.

261 Officer Patrick Marco, La Crosse Police Department, official police report, Case #06-47087, October 3, 2006.

262 Detective M Blokhuis, La Crosse Police Department, official police report, Case #06-47087, October 4, 2006, pp. 11-12.

263 Investigator C. Jobolski, La Crosse Police Department, official police report, Case #06-

47087, September 30, 2006, p. 2.

264   Investigator M. Byerson, La Crosse Police Department, official police report, Case #06-47087, September 30, 2006, p. 5.

265   Ibid., p. 2.

266   Ibid., p. 3.

267   Ibid.

268   Ibid.

269   Ibid., p. 4.

270   Ibid.

271   *Advance-Titan* (Oshkosh, WI), October 5, 2006, p. A4.

272   Ibid.

273   Ibid.

274   Ibid.

275   Ibid.

276   *Wisconsin State Journal*, October 15, 2005, p. D3.

277   Ibid.

278   *Green Bay Press-Gazette*, November 1, 2006, p. 10.

279   William Wilcoxen, "Minneapolis Police Apologize, say Student's Death a Homicide," *Minnesota Public Radio*, November 21, 2006, http://www.mprnews.org/story/2006/11/20/jenkins (accessed December 29, 2016).

280   Ibid.

281   *Pioneer Press* (St. Paul, MN), August 1, 2007, p. 1.

282   Ibid.

283   Footprints at the River's Edge, "Chris Jenkins Homicide: Someone Knows Something," http://footprintsattheriversedge.blogspot.com/2013/11/chris-jenkins-homicide-someone-knows.html (accessed December 29, 2016).

284   Dallas S. Drake, Cheryl M. Bebernes, Brandon J. Wheeler, Eden Z. Stelflug, Peter D. Espenson, Angela M. Van Auken, Kevin R. Olson, Agathe M. Panaretos, & Ben J. Anderson, "Drowning the Smiley Face Murder Theory," Center from Homicide Research, 2010, http://homicidecenter.org/wp-content/uploads/2012/03/Research-Brief-on-Smiley-Face-Murder-Theory-FINAL.pdf (accessed December 29, 2016).

285   Ibid.

286   *Asbury Park Press* (Asbury Park, NJ), September 4, 2007, p. 9.

287 Ibid.

288 Eugene Kane, The Killer Nobody wants to Talk About," *OnMilwaukee.com*, April 3, 2013, http://onmilwaukee.com/buzz/articles/smileyfacekiler.html (accessed December 30, 2016).

289 Investigator J. Rindfleisch, La Crosse Police Department, official police report, Case #07-44709, September 30, 2007, p. 3.

290 Ibid.

291 Ibid.

292 Ibid.

293 Ibid, p. 1.

294 Ibid., p. 2; Officer A. Rosenow, La Crosse Police Department, official police report, Case #07-44709, September 30, 2007, p. 1.

295 Ibid.

296 Investigator C. Joholski, La Crosse Police Department, official police report, Case #07-44709, September 30, 2007, p. 5.

297 Footprints at the River's Edge, "09/30/07: Christopher Melancon, 24, La Crosse, WI," http://footprintsattheriversedge.blogspot.com/2007/10/093007-christopher-melancon-24.html (accessed December 30, 2016); Investigator C. Joholski, La Crosse Police Department, official police report, Case #07-44709, September 30, 2007, p. 6.

298 *Pioneer Press* (St. Paul), October 2, 2007, p. 1B.

299 *Milwaukee Journal Sentinel*, October 2, 2007, p. 3B.

300 Kim McDarison, "Coincidence? A Decade of College Student Drowning Deaths comes to the Fore with Discovery of UW-Milwaukee student Nick Wilcox's Body," *The Wisconsin Happy Farm*, March 29, 2013, http://wisconsinhappyfarm.com/coincidence-a-decade-of-college-student-drowning-deaths-comes-to-the-fore-with-discovery-of-uw-milwaukee-student-nick-wilcoxs-body/ (accessed January 1, 2017).

301 Ibid.

302 Johnny Cash, *"The Ballad of Ira Hayes," Google Play Music*, https://play.google.com/music/preview/Tknrvvwpaobc4qfrp4faabqbxiq?lyrics=1&utm_source=google&utm_medium=search&utm_campaign=lyrics&pcampaignid=kp-lyrics (accessed January 1, 2017); Arlington National Cemetery, "Ira Hamilton Hayes," http://www.arlingtoncemetery.net/ira-hayes.htm (accessed January 1, 2017); Arizona Daily Star (Tucson, AZ), January 25, 1955, p. 1.

303 Jeffrey M. Liepitz, "Case Search Results," Wisconsin Circuit Court Access (held by author); Officer Scott Houston, Mosinee Police Department, official police report, Case #08-75, March 24, 2008, p. 3.

304 Officer Jeffrey Stankowski, Mosinee Police Department, official police report, Case #08-75, March 24, 2008, p. 1.

305 Ibid.

306 Ibid., pp. 1 & 2; Report of Amber Stanley, Mosinee PD Case #08-75, February 12, 2008, p. 1.

307 Officer Jeffrey Stankowski, Mosinee Police Department, official police report, Case #08-75, March 24, 2008, p. 2.

308 Ibid.

309 Officer Timothy Westergard, Mosinee Police Department, official police report, Case #08-75, March 24, 2008, pp. 1 & 2.

310 Ibid., p. 2.

311 Ibid.

312 Ibid.

313 Officer Timothy Westergard, Mosinee Police Department, official police report, Case #08-75, March 24, 2008, p. 2.

314 Ibid., p. 3.

315 Ibid., p. 4.

316 Ibid.

317 Ibid., p. 5.

318 Ibid., p. 6; Footprints on the River's Edge, "02/10/08: Jeffrey Liepitz, 35, Mosinee, WI," http://footprintsattheriversedge.blogspot.com/2010/09/021008-jeffrey-liepitz-35-mosinee-wi.html (accessed January 4, 2017).

319 Officer Timothy Westergard, Mosinee Police Department, official police report, Case #08-75, March 24, 2008, p. 6; Report of Marathon County Medical Examiner Larson, March 19, 2008.

320 Ibid., AIT Laboratories, Specimen #40072732, report completed on March 28, 2008.

321 *Wisconsin State Journal*, March 18, 2008, p. C3.

322 Mike Celizic, "The (Smiley) Face of a Killer?" April 29, 2008, *Today.com*, http://www.today.com/news/smiley-face-killer-wbna24366804 (accessed January 4, 2017).

323 Ibid.

324 Ibid.; Bill Hewitt, "Are Serial Killers Stalking College Men?" People Magazine, May 12, 2008, http://people.com/archive/are-serial-killers-stalking-college-men-vol-69-no-18/ (accessed January 4, 2017); Detective Eric Larsen, Eau Claire Police Department, official police report, Case #1-05-012916, May 1, 2008, p. 1

325 Randi Kaye, "Smiley Face Killers may be Stalking College Men," CNN, May 21, 2008, http://www.cnn.com/2008/CRIME/05/21/smiley.face.killer/ (accessed January 4, 2017).

326 Detective Eric Larsen, Eau Claire Police Department, official police report, Case #01-05-012916, April 30, 2008, p. 1.

327 "What is the victim precipitation theory?" Referene.com, https://www.reference.com/world-view/victim-precipitation-theory-c54217b4b416742e# (accessed January 7, 2017).

328 Officer G. Fifarek, Green Bay Police Department, official police report, Case #09-205733, April 30, 2009, p. 1; Detective B. Biller, Green Bay Police Department, official police report, Case #09-205733, June 24, 2009.

329 Ibid.;

330 Ibid.

331 Detective B. Biller, Green Bay Police Department, official police report, interview of Lori Van Essen, Case #09-205733, April 24, 2009, p. 2.

332 Ibid.

333 Officer G. Fifarek, Green Bay Police Department, official police report, Case #09-205733, April 30, 2009, p. 1.

334 Ibid.

335 Ibid., p. 2.

336 Glenn J. Spevacek, written statement to Green Bay police, Case #09-205733, April 24, 2009.

337 Officer Gerarden, Green Bay Police Department, official police report, Case #09-205733, April 24, 2009, p. 1; Detective G. Deviley, Green Bay Police Department, official police report, Case #09-205733, April 25, 2009; Detective B. Biller, Green Bay Police Department, official police report, Case #09-205733, April 24, 2009, p. 1.

338 Ibid., p. 2.

339 Detective G. Deviley, Green Bay Police Department, official police report, Case #09-205733, April 25, 2009; Detective B. Biller, Green Bay Police Department, official police report, Case #09-205733, April 24, 2009, p. 1; Detective B. Biller, Green Bay Police Department, official police report, Case #09-205733, May 26, 2009.

340 "Hours to Zero BAC," SelfCounseling.com, http://www.selfcounseling.com/help/alcohol/hourstozerobac.html (accessed January 8, 2017); Detective B. Biller, Green Bay Police Department, official police report, Case #09-205733, April 25, 2009.

341 Ibid.

342 Detective G. Deviley, Green Bay Police Department, official police report, interview of Thomas Malecki, Case #09-205733, April 25, 2009.

343 Officer G. Fifarek, Green Bay Police Department, official police report, Case #09-205733, April 30, 2009, p. 2.

344 Detective B. Biller, Green Bay Police Department, official police report, Case #09-205733, May 4, 2009.

345 Ibid.

346 Detective B. Biller, Green Bay Police Department, official police report, Case #09-205733, June 24, 2009.

347 Ibid.

348 Detective B. Biller, Green Bay Police Department, official police report, Case #09-205733, May 4, 2009; Cellular Telephone records of Kimberly Stiles, Log #117, #119-122, April 5, 2009 (held by author).

349 Detective B. Biller, Green Bay Police Department, official police report, Case #09-205733, July 27, 2009.

350 Footprints at the River's Edge, "04/04/09: Jesse Archer, 33, Green Bay, WI," http://footprintsattheriversedge.blogspot.com/2009/04/body-of-missing-green-bay-man-found-in.html (accessed January 10, 2017).

351 Geoscience News and Information, "Wisconsin Lakes, Rivers and Water Resources," http://geology.com/lakes-rivers-water/wisconsin.shtml (accessed January 10, 2017); Breann Schossow and Ashley Krautkramer, "Wisconsin vs. Minnesota: Lakes," *UW-Eau Claire Spectator*, March 4, 2010, http://www.spectatornews.com/currents/2010/03/04/wisconsin-vs-minnesota-lakes/ (accessed January 10, 2017); Associated Press, New Mexico's Annual Tragedies: Dying Cold, Alone and Drunk in a Field," cbsnews.com, December 22, 2015, http://www.cbsnews.com/news/alcoholism-hypothermia-deadly-recurring-navajo-new-mexico/ (accessed January 10, 2017).

352 Ibid.

353 Deputy Chris Kowalczyk, Chippewa County Sheriff's Department, official police report, Case #09-16108, November 8, 2009, p. 3; Footprints at the River's Edge, "11/01/09: Russell Plummer, 20, Bloomer, WI," http://footprintsattheriversedge.blogspot.com/2011/02/110109-russell-plummer-20-bloomer-wi.html (accessed January 12, 2017).

354 Deputy Mitchell Gibson, Chippewa County Sheriff's Department, official police report, Case #09-16108, November 10, 2009, pp. 1 & 2.

355 Investigator Bradely Lau, Chippewa County Sheriff's Department, official police report, Case #09-16108, November 10, 2009, pp. 1 & 2.

356 Ibid., p. 2.

357 Ibid.

358 Ibid.

359 Investigator Michael Stangl, Chippewa County Sheriff's Department, official police report, Case #09-16108, November 11, 2009, pp. 1 & 2; Investigator Richard Price, Chippewa County Sheriff's Department, official police report, Case #09-16108, p. 1.

360 Investigator Bradely Lau, Chippewa County Sheriff's Department, official police report, Case #09-16108, November 12, 2009.

361 Investigator Bradely Lau, Chippewa County Sheriff's Department, official police report, Case #09-16108, November 10, 2009, p. 2.

362 John Hopkins Medicine, "Health Library: Traumatic Brain Injury," John Hopkins Medicine, http://www.hopkinsmedicine.org/healthlibrary/conditions/physical_medicine_and_re-

habilitation/acquired_brain_injury_85,P01145/ (accessed January 13, 2017).

363 Kirk Olson, Examination report: Russell Plummer's cellular telephone, November 12, 2009; Investigator Richard Price, Chippewa County Sheriff's Department, official police report, Case #09-16108, November 12, 2009, p. 1; *Eau Claire Leader-Telegram*, November 10, 2009, p. 3.

364 Investigator Richard Price, Chippewa County Sheriff's Department, official police report, Case #09-16108, March 11, 2010, pp. 2 & 3; Investigator Richard Price, Chippewa County Sheriff's Department, official police report, Case #09-16108, March 31, 2010, p. 2.

365 WQOW News, "A Family's Search: What happened to Russell Plummer?" WQOW. com, November 16, 2010, http://www.wqow.com/story/13515463/one-year-later-family-still-searching-for-answer-to-accidental-death (accessed January 16, 2017).

366 Ibid.

367 Mark Gunderman, "Family still Looking for Answers in Young Soldier's Death," *Chippewa Herald*, April 20, 2012, http://chippewa.com/news/local/family-still-looking-for-answers-in-young-soldier-s-death/article_6c770a94-8b05-11e1-ad4a-0019bb2963f4.html (accessed January 16, 2017).

368 Ibid.; *Wisconsin State Journal*, April 22, 2012, p. C2.

369 Investigator Richard Price, Chippewa County Sheriff's Department, official police report, Case #09-16108, March 11, 2010, pp. 2 & 3.

370 Captain Chad La Lor, Superior Police Department, New Release, May 14, 2010.

371 *Minneapolis Star-Tribune*, February 2, 1994, p. 24; Footprints at the River's Edge, "01/17/10: Sylvester McCurry Jr., 18, Superior, WI," http://footprintsattheriversedge.blogspot. com/2010/01/011609-sylvester-mccurry-superior-wi.html (accessed January 23, 2017).

372 Ibid.; *Duluth News-Tribune*, January 30, 2010, p. 5.

373 Footprints at the River's Edge, "01/17/10: Sylvester McCurry Jr., 18, Superior, WI," http://footprintsattheriversedge.blogspot.com/2010/01/011609-sylvester-mccurry-superior-wi.html (accessed January 23, 2017).

374 Detective Jack Curphy, Superior Police Department, official police report, Case #1001068, May 25, 2010, p. 2.

375 Ibid., p. 3.

376 Ibid.

377 Footprints at the River's Edge, "01/17/10: Sylvester McCurry Jr., 18, Superior, WI," http://footprintsattheriversedge.blogspot.com/2010/01/011609-sylvester-mccurry-superior-wi.html (accessed January 23, 2017).

378 Ibid.; Captain Chad La Lor, Superior Police Department, New Release, May 14, 2010.

379 Officer Andrew Angst, La Crosse Police Department, official police report, Case 10-10-6481, February 14, 2010, p. 3; Footprints at the River's Edge, "02/14/10: Craig Meyers, 21, La Crosse, WI," http://footprintsattheriversedge.blogspot.com/2010/02/021410-craig-meyers-

21-la-crosse-wi.html (accessed January 30, 2017).

380   Officer Andrew Angst, La Crosse Police Department, official police report, Case 10-10-6481, February 14, 2010, p. 1.

381   Officer Phil Martin, La Crosse Police Department, official police report, Case 10-10-6481, February 14, 2010, p. 1.

382   Detective S. Kudron, La Crosse Police Department, official police report, Case 10-10-6481, February 17, 2010, p. 3.

383   Ibid., p. 4.

384   Sergeant Michael Blokhuis, La Crosse Police Department, official police report, Case 10-10-6481, February 16, 2010, pp. 1 & 2.

385   Investigator M. Malott, La Crosse Police Department, official police report, Case 10-10-6481, February 19, 2010, p. 2.

386   Investigator S. Kudron, La Crosse Police Department, official police report, Case 10-10-6481, February 19, 2010, p. 1; *La Crosse Tribune*, February 19, 2010, p. 1.

387   Ibid.

388   Mary Rinzel, "New Information: Police Chief Speaks out Against Serial Killer Theory," WEAU.com, February 19, 2010, http://www.weau.com/home/headlines/84754187.html (accessed January 30, 2017).

389   Officer L. Ristau, Superior Police Department, official police report, Case #10-08626, May 22, 2010.

390   Deputy M. Fritz, Douglas County Sheriff's Department, official police report, Case 10-3263, May 22, 2010, p. 1; Sergeant Derrick Hughes, Superior Police Department, official police report, Case #10-08626, May 22, 2010, p. 1.

391   Duluth News Tribune, "Family told Body Found Saturday is Sylvester McCurry," *duluthnewstribune.com*, May 23, 2010, http://www.duluthnewstribune.com/content/family-told-body-found-saturday-sylvester-mccurry (accessed May 23, 2010).

392   Detective Cory Hanson, Superior Police Department, official police report, Case #10-08626, May 25, 2010, pp. 1 & 2.

393   Captain Chad La Lor, Superior Police Department, official police report, Case #10-08626, May 26, 2010.

394   Ibid., p. 2.

395   Captain Chad La Lor, Superior Police Department, official police report, Case #10-08626, August 13, 2010.

396   Katherine Ramsland, "Serial Killer Signatures," *Psychologytoday.com*, December 4, 2013, https://www.psychologytoday.com/blog/shadow-boxing/201312/serial-killer-signatures (accessed February 2, 2017).

397   Scott A. Bonn, "Serial Killers: Modus Operandi, Signature, Staging & Posing," *Psycholo-*

gytoday.com, June 29, 2015, https://www.psychologytoday.com/blog/wicked-deeds/201506/serial-killers-modus-operandi-signature-staging-posing (accessed February 2, 2017).

398   Detective Claire McCoy, Madison Police Department, official police reports, Case #10-343991, December 4, 2010; Deputy Max Jenatscheck, Columbia County Sheriff's Department, official police reports, Case #11-10112, March 28, 2011; Bill Novak, "Police Seeking Clues to Man Missing for Two Weeks," *Madison.com*, December 15, 2010, http://host.madison.com/ct/news/local/crime_and_courts/police-seeking-clues-to-man-missing-for-two-weeks/article_be71f80c-085e-11e0-8b8a-001cc4c03286.html (accessed February 2, 2010); Detective Greg Bisch, Columbia County Sheriff's Department, official police reports, Case #11-10112, March 28, 2011, p. 8.

399   Daniel E. Hall, *Criminal Law and Procedure* (Clifton Park, NY: Cengage Learning, 2014, 7th ed.), 493.

400   "Missing Madison Man Could Be In Dodge County," *WXRO Radio*, January 27, 2011, http://wxroradio.blogspot.com/2011/01/top-stories-january-27th.html (accessed February 3, 2017); Sarah Rackley Olson, Using Cell Tower Data to Track a Suspect's Location," Forensic Resources, July 2, 2014, https://ncforensics.wordpress.com/2014/07/02/using-cell-tower-data-to-track-a-suspects-location/ (accessed February 3, 2017).

401   Nate Elsas, "Please Help! My Roommate Joseph Sjoberg is Missing. Please Help!," Reddit.com, submitted six years ago (held by author).

402   Ibid.

403   Deputy Max Jenatscheck, Columbia County Sheriff's Department, official police reports, Case #11-10112, March 28, 2011.

404   Ibid.

405   Detective Greg Bisch, Columbia County Sheriff's Department, official police reports, Case #11-10112, March 28, 2011, p. 1.

406   Ibid., pp. 2 & 3.

407   Detective Greg Bisch, Columbia County Sheriff's Department, official police reports, Case #11-10112, March 28, 2011, p. 7.

408   Detective Greg Bisch, Columbia County Sheriff's Department, official police reports, Case #11-10112, April 16, 2011.

409   Evelyn Kwong, "Intoxicated Man Arrested after getting into Police Car," *Toronto Star*, August 7, 2016, https://www.thestar.com/news/crime/2016/08/07/intoxicated-man-arrested-after-getting-into-police-car.html (accessed February 14, 2017); "Drunk Man Wanders onto Runway at Sky Harbor Airport," *CBS58az.com*, November 16, 2016, http://www.cbs5az.com/story/33728593/drunk-man-wanders-onto-runway-at-sky-harbor-airport (accessed February 14, 2017).

410   Detective Roger Craig, Walworth County Sheriff's Department, official police report, Case #11-11034, June 9, 2011; Footprints on the River's Edge, "05/28/11: Mark Wegener, 20, Whitewater, WI," http://footprintsattheriversedge.blogspot.com/2011/06/052811-mark-wegener-20-whitewater-wi.html (accessed February 14, 2017).

411 "UPDATE: Body Of Missing Man Found," *nbc15.com*, May 30, 2011, http://www.nbc15.com/home/headlines/Whitewater_Police_Search_for_Missing_Man_122800184.html (accessed February 15, 2017).

412 Detective Kilpin, Walworth County Sheriff's Department, official police report, Case #11-15237, May 30, 2011.

413 UW-Whitewater Confessions, "Everyone Needs to Read this Post," *Facebook.com*, March 3, 2013 (held by author).

414 Ibid.

415 Detective Banaszynski, Walworth County Sheriff's Department, official police report, Case #11-15233, May 31, 2011, p. 3.

416 Ibid., p. 2.

417 Detective Robert Craig, Walworth County Sheriff's Department, official police report, Case #11-15237, May 31, 2011; "Death of UW-Whitewater Student Ruled Accidental," The Royal Purple (UW-Whitewater), August 4, 2011, http://royalpurplenews.com/2808/news/top-news/death-of-uw-whitewater-student-ruled-accidental/ (accessed February 15, 2017).

418 UW-Whitewater Confessions, "Everyone Needs to Read this Post," *Facebook.com*, March 3, 2013 (held by author).

419 Detective Robert Craig, Walworth County Sheriff's Department, official police report, Case #11-15237, June 15, 2011.

420 Oliva B. Waxman, "Brooklyn Man Electrocuted after Urinating on Subway's 'Third Rail,'" *Time.com*, July 8, 2013, http://newsfeed.time.com/2013/07/08/brooklyn-man-electrocuted-after-urinating-on-subways-third-rail/ (accessed February 17, 2017).

421 The Life Saving Society, "Boating and Fishing Safety Tips," *lifesaving.ca*, http://www.lifesaving.ca/what-we-do/water-smart-public-education/boating-fishing-safety-tips/ (accessed February 17, 2017).

422 The Dominion Post, "Man Drowned Urinating off Boat," *Stuff.co.nz*, November 30, 2012, http://www.stuff.co.nz/dominion-post/news/porirua/8019721/Man-drowned-urinating-off-boat (accessed February 17, 2017).

423 Officer Tim Porn, Eau Claire Police Department, official police report, Case #11-017771, September 2, 2011.

424 Sergeant Greg Weber, Eau Claire Police Department, official police report, Case #11-017771, September 2, 2011, p. 1; Dr. Robert V. Ridenour, III, Sacred Heart Hospital, Autopsy Report, Case #A11-116, September 6, 2011, p. 5.

425 Detective Michael Glennon, Eau Claire Police Department, official police report, Case #11-017771, September 3, 2011.

426 Detective Michael Glennon, Eau Claire Police Department, official police report, Case #11-017771, September 6, 2011.

427 Detective Michael Glennon, Eau Claire Police Department, official police report, Case

#11-017771, September 18, 2011.

428   Ibid.; Kathlyn Hotynski, "The Best of Eau Claire 2006-2007," *The Spectator* (UW-Eau Claire Student Newspaper), May 10, 2007, http://www.spectatornews.com/showcase/2007/05/10/the-best-of-eau-claire-2006-2007/ (accessed February 18, 2017).

429   Detective Michael Glennon, Eau Claire Police Department, official police report, Case #11-017771, September 9, 2011.

430   Ibid.

431   Detective Michael Glennon, Eau Claire Police Department, official police report, Case #11-017771, September 6, 2011; Ibid, September 9, 2011.

432   Detective Michael Glennon, Eau Claire Police Department, official police report, Case #11-017771, September 15, 2011.

433   Deputy J. Sander, St. Croix County Sheriff's Office, official police report, Case #11-10393, December 6, 2011, p. 1.

434   Ibid.

435   Ibid.

436   Jackie Grumish, "NR Man's Body Found in the Willow River," *Rivertowns.net*, December 6, 2011, http://www.rivertowns.net/content/nr-mans-body-found-willow-river (accessed February 20, 2017).

437   Deputy Standaert, St. Croix County Sheriff's Office, official police report, Case #11-10393, December 6, 2011.

438   Ibid.; Investigator Dean Fayerweather, St. Croix County Sheriff's Office, official police report, Case #11-10393, December 6, 2011.

439   Ibid.; Wisconsin State Laboratory of Hygiene, Hudson, WI, Specimen #11FX02090, December 12, 2011.

440   Jeremy Gillis, St. Croix County, "In RE: the Support/Maintenance of K J G," Case #2011FA000035, https://wcca.wicourts.gov/caseDetails.do;jsessionid=1920DFC0C8D90F45 8874A7944907E3D9.render6?caseNo=2011FA000035&countyNo=55&cacheId=7A65D536 26A050B2D6BA911CA5A4C44E&recordCount=2&offset=1 (accessed February 19, 2017).

441   Officer Mathew Ziegler, Oshkosh Police Department, official police report, Case #OP12-000924, January 8, 2012, p. 1.

442   Detective Brett Robinson, Oshkosh Police Department, official police report, Case #OP12-000924, January 16, 2012.

443   Officer Mathew Ziegler, Oshkosh Police Department, official police report, Case #OP12-000924, January 8, 2012, p. 1.

444   Ibid.; Detective Jeremy Krueger, Oshkosh Police Department, official police report, Case #OP12-000924, January 9, 2012, p. 1.

445   Detective Brett Robinson, Oshkosh Police Department, official police report, Case

#OP12-000924, January 10, 2012, p. 1.

446 Detective Jeremy Krueger, Oshkosh Police Department, official police report, Case #OP12-000924, January 9, 2012, p. 1.

447 Officer Mathew Ziegler, Oshkosh Police Department, official police report, Case #OP12-000924, January 8, 2012, p. 2.

448 Detective Brett Robinson, Oshkosh Police Department, official police report, Case #OP12-000924, January 10, 2012, p. 2; *Philadelphia Daily News*, January 10, 2012, p. 42.

449 Ibid.; Detective Brett Robinson, Oshkosh Police Department, official police report, Case #OP12-000924, January 9, 2012, p. 3.

450 *Milwaukee Journal Sentinel,* March 7, 2012, 3B; Detective Brett Robinson, Oshkosh Police Department, official police report, Case #OP12-000924, March 7, 2012.

451 Patricia C. Rutledge, Aesoon Park and Kenneth J. Sher, "21st Birthday Drinking: Extremely Extreme," *Journal of Consulting and Clinical Psychology*, 2008, Vol.76 (3).

452 Officer Aimee Kontos, Stevens Point Police Department, official police report, Case #C12-03613, March 3, 2012, p. 1.

453 Ibid.

454 Ibid., p. 8.

455 Ibid.

456 Detective Sergeant Tony Babi, Stevens Point Police Department, official police report, Case #C12-03613, March 4, 2012, p. 1.

457 Ibid., p. 2.

458 Officer Aimee Kontos, Stevens Point Police Department, official police report, Case #C12-03613, March 3, 2012, p. 4.

459 Ibid., p. 6.

460 Ibid.

461 Detective Sergeant Tony Babi, Stevens Point Police Department, official police report, Case #C12-03613, March 4, 2012, p. 4.

462 Ibid., pp. 4 & 6.

463 Ibid.

464 Ibid., p. 7.

465 Ibid.

466 *Wisconsin State Journal*, March 6, 2012, A3.

154

467   Satoshi Kanazawa, "Why Intelligent People Use More Drugs," *Psychology Today*, November 1, 2010, https://www.psychologytoday.com/blog/the-scientific-fundamentalist/201010/why-intelligent-people-use-more-drugs (accessed February 27, 2017).

468   Report filed by Officer #406, Whitewater Police Department, official police report, Case #12-1744, July 28, 2012, pp. 1 & 2.

469   Officer Thomas Kleinfeldt, Whitewater Police Department, official police report, Case #12-1744, July 30, 2012, p. 1.

470   Ibid.

471   Ibid, pp. 2 & 3.

472   Ibid., p. 2.

473   Detective Vander Steeg, Whitewater Police Department, official police report, Case #12-1744, July 30, 2012, p. 3.

474   Officer Thomas Kleinfeldt, Whitewater Police Department, official police report, Case #12-1744, July 30, 2012, p. 2.

475   Officer Becker, Whitewater Police Department, official police report, Case #12-1744, July 28, 2012, p. 1.

476   Ibid.

477   Report filed by Officer #406, Whitewater Police Department, official police report, Case #12-1744, July 28, 2012, p. 1.

478   Ibid., p. 2.

479   Detective Flaherty, Whitewater Police Department, official police report, Case #12-1744, July 31, 2012, p. 1.

480   Officer Badge #409, Whitewater Police Department, official police report, Case #12-1744, July 29, 2012, p. 3.

481   "A Family's Unanswered Questions," *The Royal Purple News* (UW-Whitewater), October 30, 2012, http://royalpurplenews.com/8717/news/a-familys-unanswered-questions/ (accessed February 27, 2017); Whitewater Police Department, Permission to Search Private Premises and/or Motor Vehicle, Signed by Michael Schildt, July 29, 2012.

482   "A Family's Unanswered Questions," The Royal Purple News (UW-Whitewater), October 30, 2012, http://royalpurplenews.com/8717/news/a-familys-unanswered-questions/ (accessed February 27, 2017.

483   Whitewater Police Department, Missing Person's Poster, Benjamin Fuder, July 28, 2012.

484   Ibid.

485   Mike Riggs, "An Ex-Cop's Guide to Not Getting Arrested," *CityLab.com*, November 7, 2013, http://www.citylab.com/navigator/2013/11/ex-cops-guide-not-getting-arrested/7491/ (accessed February 27, 2017).

155

486 "Back Road Drunks — Don't Try to Avoid Police in Virginia," The Bluefield Daily Telegraph (Bluefield, VA), August 22, 2008, http://www.bdtonline.com/opinion/editorials/back-road-drunks-don-t-try-to-avoid-police-in/article_bf5b6e8c-5845-51e3-8d4f-3424856eefa9.html (accessed February 27, 2017).

487 *State of Wisconsin v. Shalim Shah Augustine*, La Crosse County Case #2014-TR003514 (held by author).

488 Investigator Linnea Miller, La Crosse Police Department, official police report, Case #10-14-32483, July 11, 2014, p. 1.

489 Officer Curns, La Crosse Police Department, official police report, Case #10-14-32483, July 9, 2014, p. 1.

490 Investigator Linnea Miller, La Crosse Police Department, official police report, Case #10-14-32483, July 11, 2014, pp. 1 & 2.

491 Ibid., p. 3.

492 Ibid.

493 Officer Curns, La Crosse Police Department, official police report, Case #10-14-32483, July 9, 2014, p. 2.

494 Investigator Timothy O'Neill, La Crosse Police Department, official police report, Case #10-14-32483, July 17, 2014, p. 2.

495 Officer Andrew Rosenow, La Crosse Police Department, official police report, Case #10-14-32483, July 11, 2014, p. 1.

496 Investigator Timothy O'Neill, La Crosse Police Department, official police report, Case #10-14-32483, July 17, 2014, p. 4.

497 Ibid., p. 5.

498 Ibid, p. 5; WIZM Staff, "Augustine Tox Results Back," *WIZM.com*, August 13, 2014, http://www.1410wizm.com/index.php/item/23846-augustine-tox-results-back (accessed February 27, 2107).

499 Investigator Timothy O'Neill, La Crosse Police Department, official police report, Case #10-14-32483, July 17, 2014, p. 5.

500 Officer Curns, La Crosse Police Department, official police report, Case #10-14-32483, July 9, 2014, p. 2.

501 Investigator Linnea Miller, La Crosse Police Department, official police report, Case #10-14-32483, July 11, 2014, p. 2.

502 "Hypothermia-Related Mortality --- Montana, 1999—2004," Center for Disease Control, April 20, 2007, https://www.cdc.gov/mmwr/preview/mmwrhtml/mm5615a3.htm (accessed February 27, 2017).

503 Ibid.

INDEX

160

Made in the USA
Lexington, KY
07 December 2018